# BEYOND THE WALL OF RESISTANCE

Also by Rick Maurer

*Feedback Toolkit*
*Caught in the Middle*

# BEYOND THE WALL OF RESISTANCE

## UNCONVENTIONAL STRATEGIES THAT BUILD SUPPORT FOR CHANGE

## RICK MAURER

### Bard Books, Inc.
Austin, Texas

# BEYOND THE WALL OF RESISTANCE

UNCONVENTIONAL STRATEGIES THAT BUILD SUPPORT FOR CHANGE

Bard Press
1515 Capital of Texas Hwy. South
Suite 205
Austin, Texas 78746
(512) 329-8373 Phone
(512) 329-6051 Fax
www.bardpress.com

## ORDERING INFORMATION

To order additional copies, contact your local bookstore or call 1-800-945-3132.
Quantity discounts are available.

ISBN      1-885167-07-5          hardcover

*Library of Congress Cataloging-in-Publication Data*
Maurer, Rick.
     Beyond the wall of resistance : unconventional strategies that
  build support for change / Rick Maurer.
       p.    cm.
  Includes bibliographical references and index.
    ISBN 1-885167-07-5 (hardcover)
    1. Organizational change—Management.  2. Strategic planning.
  I.Title.
HD58.8.M3323  1996                          95-36774
658.4'06—dc20                               CIP

*The author may be contacted at:*

Maurer & Associates
(703) 525-7074 *phone*
(703) 525-0183 *fax*
www.beyondresistance.com *website*
rmaurer@beyondresistance.com *e-mail*

## CREDITS

*Executive editor:* Leslie Stephen
*Copyediting:* Jeff Morris
*Proofreading:* Deborah Costenbader, Leslie Coplin
*Jacket design:* Archetype, Inc.
*Text design/production:* Archetype, Inc.
*Index:* Linda Webster

First printing, January 1996
Second printing, March 1996
Third printing, November 1998

*Dedicated to the memory of my sister,
Laraine, who faced massive change in her life
with grace, courage, and good humor*

# TABLE OF CONTENTS

About the Author ........................................................*13*
Acknowledgments .....................................................*14*

**PART  I    RESISTANCE AND CHANGE**

Chapter 1   The Power of Resistance ........................................*17*
  - *Failed Dreams*
  - *The Human Toll*
  - *The Challenge*
  - *In This Book*
  - *The Value of Working with Resistance*

Chapter 2   The Nature of Resistance ..........................................*23*
  - *What Is Resistance?*
  - *How to Recognize Resistance*
  - *Anticipating Resistance*
  - *The Cycle of Change*

Chapter 3   Making Matters Worse ...............................*33*
  - *Our Strong Reaction*
  - *Our Default Positions*
  - *Why the Default Strategies Don't Work*
  - *Approaches to Change and Resistance: Conventional and Unconventional*

Chapter 4   Seeing the Potential ....................................*43*
  - *Another Stadium*
  - *Learning from Experience*
  - *Why the Unconventional Worked*
  - *A Contrast in Styles*
  - *Enter the Unknown*
  - *Two Fundamental Questions*
  - *A Third Question*
  - *Why Bother?*

NATURAL CHANGE ............................................................50
■ *An Interview with* **Margaret Wheatley**

Chapter 5     Getting Beyond the Wall .................................53
■ *Touchstone No. 1: Maintain Clear Focus*
■ *Touchstone No. 2: Embrace Resistance*
■ *Touchstone No. 3: Respect Those Who Resist*
■ *Touchstone No. 4: Relax*
■ *Touchstone No. 5: Join with the Resistance*
■ *The Flip Side*

TAKING THEIR SIDE ........................................................62
■ *An Interview with* **Peter Block**

Chapter 6     Putting It All Together ..............................65
■ *Major Cultural Change*
■ *The Cycle*
■ *Using the Cycle to Anticipate the Future*
■ *How an Individual Can Use the Touchstones*
■ *Using the Touchstones*


PART II     ASSESS THE SITUATION

Chapter 7     Where Are You Today? ...............................75
■ *Moving Against the Tide*
■ *Moving with the Tide*
■ *Your Place on the Cycle*
■ *Using the Cycle*
■ *Who Are the Players?*

A BALANCE OF FORCES ....................................................80
■ *An Interview with* **John Carter**

Chapter 8     How Intense Is the Resistance? ...............87
■ *Level 1: The Idea Itself*
■ *Level 2: Deeper Issues*
■ *Level 3: Deeply Embedded*
■ *Interplay of the Levels*

- *Beginning the Conversation*
- *Interpretation*
- *Support for Change Questionnaire*

THE HAND ON THE OTHER SIDE
OF THE WALL ....................................................................*100*
- *An Interview with Adrienne Kaufmann
  and Mary Jacksteit*

Chapter 9    What's Your Contribution
to the Problem? .....................................................*107*
- *Personal Resistance Style*
- *The Key Questions*
- *Almost Time to Engage*

THE UNSPOKEN GAME ...............................................*116*
- *An Interview with Geoffrey Bellman*


PART III    TAKE ACTION

Chapter 10   Create the Shift ..........................................*121*
- *The Shift*
- *What Creates a Shift?*
- *In Search of a Shift*

Chapter 11   Preempt Resistance ...................................*127*
- *The Dilemma of Trust*
- *"What If?" Scenarios*
- *Real Time Strategic Change*
- *Future Search*
- *Structured Dialogue*
- *Roll Your Own*
- *The Foundation*

Chapter 12   Unleash Its Power ....................................*139*
- *Why Unleash Resistance?*
- *Pick Up the Signs*
- *Invite the Storm*

- *Workout*
- *Principles for Unleashing*

THE POWER OF OPEN INVOLVEMENT .............................*144*
- *Interviews with Peter Johnson
  and Jack Robertson*

Chapter 13  Dig Beneath the Surface .........................................*153*
- *Listening and Probing*
- *Tools for Exploration*
- *Getting Things Up on the Table*

Chapter 14  Engage with Courage ...............................................*161*
- *Desperately Seeking Virgil*
- *Using Virgil*
- *Become Your Own Virgil*

THE CONFUSED FRIEND ...............................................*168*
- *An Interview with Tilden Edwards*

Chapter 15  Act! ...........................................................................*171*
- *Read the Signs*
- *Act!*
- *Keep Moving*
- *Plan for the Future*

TIMING .........................................................................*180*
- *An Interview with Rose Harvey*


NOTES, RESOURCES, AND TOOLS

Notes .........................................................................*185*
Resources...................................................................*193*
Tools..........................................................................*198*

Index.........................................................................*199*

## ABOUT THE AUTHOR

Rick Maurer has helped a broad range of organizations see the value and potential of resistance to change since founding his consulting firm, Maurer & Associates, in 1978.

Rick is the author of two previous books. *Caught in the Middle: A Leadership Guide for Partnership in the Workplace,* published in 1992, was hailed by *Quality Digest* as "an excellent departure point for those managers stranded somewhere between old responsibilities and their new roles." His second book, *Feedback Toolkit: 16 Tools for Better Communication in the Workplace,* is a compilation of tools and techniques developed through his consulting practice, published in 1994.

He is also a frequent and highly regarded presenter and facilitator at professional programs and conferences, including the national conventions of the Association for Quality and Participation, the American Society for Training and Development, and the Organization Development Network. For fifteen years he was on the staff of the Leadership Development Program at the University of Maryland, a program of the Center for Creative Leadership.

Rick has been quoted in *The Wall Street Journal, The Economist, Industry Week, Nation's Business*, and *Fortune*. He has appeared on CNBC and NBC Nightly News. His articles have appeared in many business and trade publications.

## ACKNOWLEDGMENTS

My thinking on resistance has been developing over many years, but it was only when I enrolled in the Organization and Systems Development Program at the Gestalt Institute of Cleveland a few years ago that I found not only a language for describing this phenomenon, but met people who had done a considerable amount of thinking on the subject. I would not have thought to write this book, nor could I have, without the profound influence and support I received from the faculty and fellow participants in that program. I am deeply indebted to those people.

Thanks to Matt Kayhoe and Max Stark, two fellow consultants who have influenced my thinking in many ways, from out-and-out, but always friendly, criticism of my ideas to lengthy explorations of the subject with me. Others whose ideas have helped me learn more about resistance are Phil Kalin, Maureen Kearney, Eleanor Hooks, Brenda Jones, Diane Johnson, Michael Matthews, Dinah Nieburg, Susan Schroeer, Neil Sklarew, and Jim Vanderbeck. Thanks to Warren Conner, a fine instructor of T'ai Chi and willing recipient of all manner of questions on the relationship of martial arts to organizational life.

In addition to many already named, I am grateful to those who read early drafts or portions of the manuscript and made helpful comments: Chip Bell, Geoff Bellman, Sam Crouse, Carol Dana, Margo Freeburg, Larry Knox, John Mariotti, Tom Martinec, Kathi Mocniak, Kathy Monte, LeRoy Pingho, Diane Porterfield, Kay Scott, Michael C. Thomas, Sherry Weinstein, and Marc Young. A special note of thanks to clients, leaders of organizations, and colleagues who met with me to talk about what they wanted to see in a book like this.

Thanks to the people who granted interviews. In most cases I was able to use only a small portion of what I gained from them, but I appreciate the fullness of their generosity. Thanks to Geoff Bellman, Peter Block, John Carter, Kathie Dannemiller, Tilden Edwards, Rose Harvey, Mary Jacksteit and Adrienne Kaufmann, Jack Robertson and Peter Johnson, and Margaret Wheatley.

A special appreciation for the fine folks at Bard Books. Ray and Scott Bard saw the potential in this book and continually offered sound advice on the business aspects of publishing. Leslie Stephen shepherded me through the writing and revisions with great care. Their combined commitment, wisdom, and excitement kept this labor of love from turning into just raw labor.

Thanks to Jodi Sleeper-Triplett, my business manager, who protected my time and ran the business so that I could actually write this book. Thanks to my wife, Kathy, who prodded me often with the question, "So, are you ever going to write this book?" And for her encouragement throughout the process. Words can hardly express my appreciation for her constant support.

When our first parents were driven out of Paradise, Adam is believed to have remarked to Eve: "My dear, we live in an age of transition."
—*William Inge*

# PART I

*Resistance*
*and Change*

# 1 THE POWER OF RESISTANCE

History teaches us that men and nations behave wisely once they have exhausted all other alternatives.
—*Abba Eban*

Resistance kills change. Every day people resist our ideas. A corporate reorganization dies of inertia. Developers and environmental groups polarize over the use of a piece of land. A middle manager is stunned to see a pet project falter when peers refuse to implement it. Even at home, arguments break out every time a parent tries to make a teenager study harder.

## FAILED DREAMS

New ideas often fail, not on their relative merits, but on how well we are able to handle resistance.

Since change—reengineering, quality improvement, reorganizations, mergers, acquisitions, downsizing, expansion, new product lines, new software, new computer systems, new procedures—is intensifying in all organizations every day, that rate of failure will continue to grow. Organizations will pay for these failed dreams in dollars and lost opportunities.

- Michael Hammer and James Champy, the authors of the bestseller *Reengineering the Corporation*, admit that they were not prepared for the massive resistance they found to reengineering.[1]

- According to research by McKinsey and Company, only 23 percent of corporate mergers recovered costs. Half of the mergers "went straight downhill," Anne B. Fisher writes in *Fortune*. "Any manager is doomed if there is no real effort beforehand to see whether the two cultures have anything in common. Yet top management too often regards cultural chemistry as a pesky detail that can safely be left to the folks in human resources."[2] As you will see, the handling of these "pesky details" must be led by the people who are leading the merger. It is far too important to delegate or take lightly.

- Senior executives in Fortune 500 companies stated that less than one-half of changes in their organizations were successful and that resistance was the main reason for the failures.[3]

- According to a study commissioned by Zenger-Miller, a major barrier to implementation of quality improvement in organizations is resistance to the change.[4] Many in the field estimate that fewer than half of these initiatives succeed.

- The Standish Group reports that development of software applications within companies enjoys a very small chance of success. Twenty-eight percent of these projects are successful in small companies, 16 percent in medium-sized organizations, and 9 percent in large companies. Many are canceled before they are completed, cost overruns plague others, and many are "no more than a mere shadow of their original specification requirements."[5]

Lack of user involvement in the early development stage is the single largest reason for these failures. In the following chapters you will read why involvement is so crucial to building support for new ideas—whether these changes are information technology, mergers, or new programs.

## THE HUMAN TOLL

If the cost of failed change is high for organizations, the cost is equally dear for people. The first casualty is trust: people start to blame one another. Too many botched plans, and people become afraid to try again. Even so-called "successful" efforts often leave a bitter taste in the mouths of those who were forced to change. The toll on individuals can be enormous.

In some organizations the pace of change is so frantic and people feel so out of control that the workplace looks like a cast party for *Night of the Living Dead:* we create zombies. Resistance in these cases comes not so much from the particular change but from the sheer immensity of what we ask of others.

We must realize that managing change means managing resistance as well. We must be able to anticipate resistance and learn to use its force to build support for change. But far too often we seem surprised when resistance appears, and not at all sure how to deal with it.

We may view resistance as a massive wall that must be destroyed so that we can get on with our work. We forget that there are people behind that wall, and when we try to destroy it, they fight back. Often our efforts succeed only in making the wall even stronger.[6]

## THE CHALLENGE

This book is an exploration of how to use the power of resistance to build support for change. It may challenge not only your view of the value of resistance but also your role as an agent of change.

Change is unsettling. It disrupts our world. Some fear they will lose status, control, even their jobs. The larger the change, the stronger the resistance. Successful change requires vision, persistence, courage, an ability to thrive on ambiguity, and a willingness to engage those who have a stake in the outcome.

The courageous face resistance and explore it. They are curious. They wonder why they are so excited, while others tremble at the mere thought of this change. They know that inside the resistance lies hope, and that if they can but unleash its energy, they will have an opportunity to build excitement for their ideas.

*Beyond the Wall of Resistance* is an exploration for me as well. I write about the subject because it intrigues and often eludes me. Resistance does not lend itself to a few easy steps. The ground continually shifts under our feet. Dealing with change and resistance is chaotic. But, I firmly believe, it is worth the effort.

Each situation is unique. On Monday, I may work brilliantly with those who resist my work. My antennae pick up the faintest signals, allowing me to explore dissatisfaction and look for common ground. On Tuesday, filled with self-assurance, I watch myself stumble and say things that add bricks to the wall. Whatever you think of resistance, working with it is seldom boring.

## IN THIS BOOK

Although the subtitle of this book is *Unconventional Strategies That Build Support for Change,* most of us already have the skills we need to work with resistance. The strategies are unconventional, not because they are new, but because they are so seldom used. The British writer G. K. Chesterton wrote, "The Christian ideal has not been tried and found wanting; it has been found difficult and left untried." These unconventional strategies sometimes can seem just as difficult. Fortunately, most of them have been tried in one way or another. It's just that most of us don't use them often or rigorously enough. My hope is that you use the ideas in this book to plan and manage change differently.

Part I of the book offers a foundation. I will explore the common approaches that seldom work, look at a more effec-

tive alternative, and introduce a model that shows how resistance and change work together.

Part II asks you to assess a current change. I encourage you to think of a particular project or idea as you read this section, and to take a few minutes to complete the assessments. This will help you test the applicability of the book. The questions raised in part II are crucial to your understanding of how to make this book practical.

In part III you will learn how to engage others. In other words, we will explore ways to put this book to work. I also include an extensive list of other resources—books, methods of study, places to study—to further your understanding of resistance.

My hope is that this book will help you see resistance in a different light and give you tools to develop strategies to embrace it.

## THE VALUE OF WORKING WITH RESISTANCE

There are many potential benefits of learning to work with resistance rather than against it:

- Using the force of resistance can increase our success rate and speed the time it takes to implement a new idea.

- Showing respect toward those who resist builds stronger relationships, not only improving the change at hand but providing a solid base for future changes.

- Working with resistance increases the likelihood that all parties can meet at least some of their goals.

Even though this book is written from front to back, and often one step follows another, the real world is far from being so orderly. William Burroughs has constructed novels by cutting his text into strips and pasting them together randomly. I was tempted to write this book the same way. (I didn't.) But dealing with resistance lends itself to Burroughs's approach. As we deal with it, we find ourselves moving forward, back, down, then up again. What seemed to be over has only just begun. As we increase resistance we find that support builds; it is a strange and paradoxical world we enter. Later in the book I use Dante's descent into the Inferno as a metaphor for this perilous and ultimately worthy journey. (After all, we must remember that Dante was on his way to Paradise.)

By the time you finish this book, I want you be excited about working with resistance. I want you to be able to embrace, rather than fear, its voice. On good days, I love resistance. It is energizing. It adds life and vibrancy to my work. It lets me know that my clients and I are alive. We are engaged. We struggle because we have a stake in the outcome.

For most, it is not easy to work with resistance, but it is doable. Perhaps your perspective will need to shift. You may need to dust off some old, seldom-used skills, and you will probably need to draw on your reserves of strength and courage; but these things are possible. You will read stories of perfectly ordinary people just like you and me who have found ways to treat resistance differently. Don't expect a magic potion or incantation; clicking your heels together three times works only in stories. Like anything important, working with resistance takes commitment and skill; but if others can do it, so can you. Don't give up hope.

- The voice of resistance can keep us from taking untimely or foolish actions.

I suspect some readers are rolling their eyes about now. It might all sound good if you had world enough and time, but this is the fast lane, where changes need to get made in a New York heartbeat.

I know this approach seems difficult. It's hard for me as well. Slowing down to go fast seems fuzzy-minded, something that doesn't have a chance to succeed in the real world. Listening to the fears and concerns of others may seem a luxury you can't afford. But consider this: Can you afford not to get others involved? Think about all the changes that fail and compare them with the ones that succeed. Think about your common reactions to resistance and consider the consequences. How have things worked out in the past? How might they have worked if you had considered some of the ideas in this book? Perhaps, just perhaps, some of the strategies in this book might have helped you roll out a new project faster; or helped keep a complex reorganization on track; or given you information that would have saved you time and money.

One form of resistance is to swallow things whole without fully digesting the information. My advice is, Chew your food. Read on with healthy skepticism. Determine which portions of *Beyond the Wall of Resistance* provide nourishment and which don't. Continually ask yourself, How will the ideas in this book help reduce resistance and increase my chances of success?

# 2 THE NATURE OF RESISTANCE

I can't understand why people are frightened of new ideas. I'm frightened of the old ones.
—*John Cage*

There is hope embedded in resistance, but to find it we must first understand what it is. Although the word is used freely when we speak of change, it is often used imprecisely. We use *resistance* to talk about some vague opposition, or we talk about those *resistors*, as if resistance were the sole province of a class of people— whom we probably don't like—known by that label. With a better understanding of the nature of resistance, you will become more adept at recognizing it in all its many forms and learn how to anticipate its occurrence.

## WHAT IS RESISTANCE?

Resistance is a force that slows or stops movement. It is a natural and expected part of change. Any system, whether the human body or an organization, resists any change that it believes will be harmful. If you have ever tried to lose weight, you will immediately recognize this dilemma. As you try to lose a few pounds, your metabolism slows to keep you from starving. Your body doesn't know that you are acting on a New Year's resolution. It is simply trying to slow you down so you can conserve energy. Research (but not personal experience) suggests that when you overeat, your metabolism speeds up to keep you at a comfortable *set point* or preferred weight. Your metabolism adjusts to keep your weight steady.

As a company begins reengineering, middle managers may resist because they feel it will harm them. They believe that they might lose their authority or even their jobs. Their *set point* is the status quo, even though they might actually *see* the need for change. This is not altogether different from standing on scales and resolving to lose those few pounds. You begin to realize that the mind and the body can work at cross purposes.

As much as you might wish for it, progress without resistance is impossible. People will always have doubts and questions. Even when you are the champion of change, you will still have doubts. Will this really work? Have I given the idea sufficient thought?

Resistance is a natural part of any change. It is also protection, energy, and a paradox.

### Protection

Resistance protects us from harm. It keeps us from skiing down treacherous double black diamond slopes after our first lesson on the bunny hill. It alerts us that taking that chair lift to Bodycast Mountain is foolhardy and hazardous to our health. In organizations, it keeps us from saying yes to every bonehead idea that some overzealous manager dreams up. By resisting, we may save ourselves lots of unnecessary work, pain, and migraines.

From the vantage point of the person resisting, caution is absolutely the right course of action. When we are the ones resisting, we see it as a positive force. It keeps us safe. Resistance can be a sign of health, a way to navigate in a complex and rapidly changing world.

If we can remember that people resist for good reasons—that they usually aren't out to get us—then we can begin to approach them differently. Keeping this thought in mind may allow us to search for ways to work with others rather than inflicting something on them.

### Energy

Resistance is energy. If you have ever faced a room full of people angry at some action you took, you will have no trouble recognizing its unique brand of energy.

The energy of resistance can be a powerful and frightening force. You may be inclined to meet this force with force. Even though you may overpower and win the battle, you will lose the war because you have lost the commitment you so desperately needed.

Your goal should be to help redirect this energy. In the martial art of Aikido, the purpose when fighting is to find harmony. When an opponent punches, the master does not counterpunch but joins the energy of the attacker's force. She might step to the side, lightly take the adversary's arm, and move with him. By blending her movement with his, she protects herself, and the opponent saves face. The master accomplishes this without kicking, taunting, or sucker punching the opponent.

### A Paradox

Pythagoras said that the world is set up in opposites—day and night, up and down, black and white. We can't know day unless we contrast it with night. The Chinese symbolize this with a circle divided into two parts, the "yin" and the "yang." Wherever I am in the circle, the opposite is still there. If you imagine that the dark portion represents change, then the white would represent resistance. They go together.

As we move within the circle, we move closer to its opposite side. (Note how black almost fades into white, and vice versa.) Change moves into resistance, resistance into change. Nothing is constant. The symbol suggests a never-ending cycle.

How to encourage movement toward change from resistance is the essence of this book. By heightening resistance, we give it so much attention that energy naturally moves to the other side. It is as if we filled the resistance side of the circle so full that energy had no place to go but to the other side.

In later chapters I will discuss ways to bring resistance out into the open. We don't do this for its own sake, but in the belief that when enough attention is paid to it, resistance usually turns to support.

The transformation from resistance to support can occur if we are willing to be part of the process. As we learn about the reasons why others resist us, we can be influenced. We begin to see the subtle interplay as they resist, we react, they resist anew. We now have a choice: we can keep sparring, or we can dance. If we choose the dance, we move back and forth, one influencing the other, until it becomes difficult to recall who resisted and who initiated.

We can influence the resistance side of the circle only if we are willing to enter it and learn from it. This means giving up our certainty. It requires suspending disbelief.

## HOW TO RECOGNIZE RESISTANCE

Archaeological remains show that when Pompeii was buried by the eruption of Mount Vesuvius in A.D. 79, villagers were caught completely by surprise. Presumably no one saw the devastating earthquake of A.D. 62 as a sign that the old volcano was still active; as a result, two thousand were killed in the eruption.[1] Today, we know the signs of an impending eruption. It is important as well to know the signs of resistance; otherwise, you risk becoming a victim of the blast.

### Confusion

Even after you have tried many times to explain the new program, people still ask basic questions: "So, why are we doing this?" "Who am I going to report to?" "How much is this going to cost?" "Where did you say you wanted to build that?" Assuming that you *did* explain things clearly, this confusion is one form of resistance.

People are not lying to us. Resistance creates an aural fog that makes it difficult for people (ourselves included) to hear what's being said. The people who best handle change patiently explain the plans over and over again. You must realize that people will begin to hear at different times and in different ways.

### Immediate Criticism

Even before people hear all the details, they express their disapproval. Groucho Marx once sang, "Whatever it is—I'm against it." This instantaneous negative reaction to you and your ideas is maddening. Have you ever worked in an organization where people routinely oppose the slightest change? Even before the idea is fully explained, they begin mounting their criticism. It is as if they have been there before and know exactly what to expect.

When individuals or groups criticize too quickly, it is likely that they have been burned before and have developed a shell of resistance. They may feel that if they allow anything through their shell, they will be hurt again.

### Denial

People put their heads in the sand and refuse to see that things are different. Often, the more you try to justify, the deeper they embed themselves.

In his PBS series *Healing and the Mind*, Bill Moyers spoke with a cardiologist who refused to admit that he had a serious heart condition. For years he refused even to look at his electrocardiogram. Our wish to not see what's in front of us can be extraordinarily strong—so strong that even a doctor who specializes in the heart won't admit the truth to himself.

### *Malicious Compliance*

People smile and appear to go along with the decision. It is only later, when they drag their feet, that you learn the truth.

The president of a small company was excited about initiating new management procedures. He was an enthusiastic champion, and no one wanted (or dared) to burst his bubble. People agreed with him in public. It took months before he realized that managers were doing only the minimum necessary to keep this change alive.

### *Sabotage*

Outright sabotage is usually easy to spot. People take strong actions that are specifically intended to stop you from proceeding. Software strangely breaks down; a machine malfunctions at an inopportune time; messages don't get delivered. If there is a positive side to sabotage, it is that there is little doubt that someone or some group is strongly opposed to your plans.

### *Easy Agreement*

People agree with you without much criticism. On the surface, this might seem ideal. You present your plan, people applaud wildly, so it seems to be time to move ahead.

Although they may sincerely wish to go along, their quick acceptance could spell disaster later, when they realize what the changes mean. They have swallowed your message whole without digesting it, like crazed young lovers who vow eternal devotion after the first date. The difference between easy agreement and malicious compliance is less in the action and more in the intent. People who give easy agreement truly believe the idea has merit. It is only later that they realize the implications of their hasty Las Vegas wedding.

ADC Kentrox, a manufacturer of telecommunications equipment, was so eager to implement ISO 9000 standards that "they almost destroyed their company."[2] They followed the ISO guidelines diligently, without adapting them to their unique organization, and created a massive bureaucratic nightmare. One senior product manager was ready to resign, believing that this "monstrosity" would kill the company. Knowing that the red tape would add months to projects, managers ignored the company's new 100-page document on ISO standards. According to David Kenney, director of quality, "We had not considered our company's situation: We are a small, market-leading company with 250 employees. We needed flexible, quickly implemented procedures—the opposite of what we had created in our attempt to please ISO's auditors. Armed with these conclusions, we restructured the new-product introduction process to include decentralization of responsibilities and a flexible approach to project management."[3]

### Deflection

People keep changing the subject. Meetings flit from topic to topic. Just as you start to talk about something of substance, someone brings up another, perhaps equally important, topic, and all attention shifts to it.

Like all other forms of resistance, deflection is a way people have of protecting themselves. Changing the subject is like raising a shield to stop an incoming arrow.

Deflection is usually unconscious and not a strategic choice. Managers in a small manufacturing plant routinely used discussions of their budget as a way of avoiding talking about other issues that affected their work.[4] It was much safer to talk about numbers than about the things they were doing to each other that inhibited productivity.

### Silence

You present your idea, the lights come up, and you look out on a corporate Mount Rushmore—chiseled stone faces giving no hint of what they think. Do people agree? Are they too stunned to speak? Are they afraid to talk?

Silence is a difficult form of resistance to address because it gives you so little to work with. And, of course, since silence sometimes does indicate support, it is hard to know what to make of it.

As a general guideline, never assume that silence means acceptance. In your own desire to get things moving you may be tempted to make that faulty assumption, only to learn later that no one was with you. Better to slow down and find out what's behind the silence.

### In-Your-Face Criticism

With no holds barred, these people tell you exactly what's on their minds. You may want to dismiss their comments because of their grating and belligerent manner, but you shouldn't. Unlike the others, these people are telling you the truth as they see it. Often they express what other, milder, souls may fear to say to you.

These people often have a reputation for their impolitic and impolite manner in the office. Since few others respect them, you may be tempted to lash out at them to make them shudder with your withering sarcasm. Don't. As soon as you do, you make it unsafe for others to speak.

Years ago I conducted a leadership development seminar for government managers. One man in the course criticized everything I said. I could see others roll their eyes when he spoke, so I thought it safe to go on the offensive. I was brilliant; Hawkeye Pierce was never so facile. My retorts were like rapiers. Surely this would shut him up and endear me to the hearts of others.

I was wrong. People sided with him. After all, he was one of their own, and I was the outsider. I spent the next two days digging myself out of the hole that I had dug for myself.

It is important to keep refining your resistance-recognizing skills. The categories listed above are valuable only as lenses through which to see its many forms. The more skilled you are at seeing it, the quicker you will be able to address it.

## ANTICIPATING RESISTANCE

Managers at Ajax Paper (a fictitious name), knowing they had to improve quality and productivity in order to survive, decided to begin an improvement process that relied on high worker involvement. The unions rebelled and closed the facility for six months.

Twenty miles away, a competitor, Beta Products, faced a similar challenge but took a radically different approach. Corporate headquarters would agree to fund capital improvements only if plant management and the six unions would agree to cooperate.

Ajax failed to anticipate the importance of support and the power of resistance. Given their history, there was no reason to believe that the unions would accept a unilateral decision that affected their members in such dramatic ways. Senior management at Beta knew better. They understood that unless they got agreement from all, the chance of success was small.

## THE CYCLE OF CHANGE

If we understand that change often follows a cyclic path, it is easier to predict potential resistance. Once we know where we are in the cycle, we begin to see options. Ajax Paper failed to grasp the cyclic nature of change; Beta embraced it.

The cycle of change can
- help us appreciate that change is cyclic and that nothing lasts forever.
- explain why resistance is occurring.
- help us predict the consequences of continuing to use the same strategies.
- point to alternatives to the current course of action.

There are six steps in the cycle: Random Incidents, Recognition, Initial Action, Implementation, Integration, and Waning Activity.

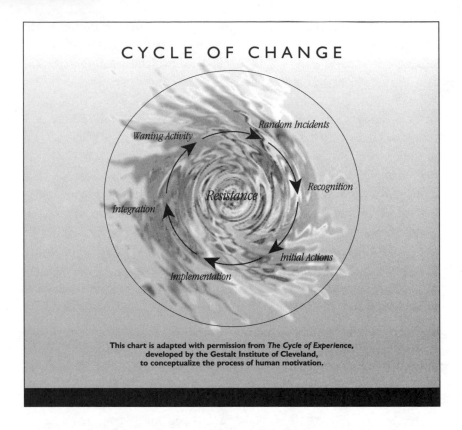

# CYCLE OF CHANGE

*Random Incidents*

*Waning Activity*

*Recognition*

*Resistance*

*Integration*

*Initial Actions*

*Implementation*

This chart is adapted with permission from *The Cycle of Experience*,
developed by the Gestalt Institute of Cleveland,
to conceptualize the process of human motivation.

### Random Incidents ("one o'clock" on the cycle)

There is very little information about the need for change. In the case of the paper plants, there may have been some reports of quality problems. When senior management realized there was a problem, most staff were still at one o'clock, unaware of the problem.

### Recognition (three o'clock)

Someone recognizes that there is a problem or an opportunity. At Beta, senior management were committed to opening the books and talking with others until most Recognized that there was indeed a problem.

Recognition is the most critical stage of the cycle. Once everyone sees the same picture of the situation, it becomes possible to get everyone aligned to move around the cycle together. Organizational consultant Kathie Dannemiller speaks about the importance of the shift that occurs when everyone Recognizes the situation. When this shift occurs, people's views are transformed. They begin to see the world from others' points of view. The shift is a realization that we are in this together. We Recognize the need for action.

### Initial Actions (five o'clock)

Once we Recognize the issue, energy builds—we want to get busy and do something. Ajax's Initial Action was unilateral. Senior management Recognized a problem and dictated a new program. They did not bother with heightening Recognition among staff. At Beta, the Initial Actions were conversations. They addressed the question, Can management and the six unions find a way to work together to save the plant? These conversations could take place only after everyone had Recognized how dire the situation was for the plant.

### Implementation (seven o'clock)

During this stage, the idea is rolled out. At Ajax, they announced the plan and tried to Implement quickly. They failed. At Beta, they ended Initial Actions by writing a document of cooperation that all parties could agree to. Implementation was based on this agreement.

### Integration (nine o'clock)

At this stage, the idea becomes part of the way we do business. Ajax never got close to this stage; Beta is working toward it. Once Beta achieves the goal, the improvement processes will no longer be special events—they will simply be the way the company does its work.

If the change were a fairy tale, this stage would end with "and they all lived happily ever after." But this is a grimmer tale, as life and the cycle move on.

### Waning Activity (eleven o'clock)

Nothing lasts forever. Even the best plans eventually run their course. Beta may find their agreement with the unions strained as they try to introduce new technology or as foreign competition demands severe cost cutting.

The transition from Integration to Waning Activity is important. Often we hang onto an old idea far too long. It's not that the idea is bad; it is simply time for the cycle to move on. IBM, once the dominant force in the computer industry, faced hard times in the early '90s. Many observers blame this on the company's inability to shift from mainframe to personal computers. According to Mark Stahlman, writing in the *Wall Street Journal,* IBM did respond to the shift in the market but failed to realize that it would take a new way of approaching the work. They failed to leave Integration and move again to the beginning of the cycle. "For a while, it looked as if IBM might be back in the lead. Through a unique combination of events, IBM hit upon the correct new idea": building alliances with others that could provide R&D and partnering with distributors instead of selling only through the company sales force. "But IBM sacrificed this lead by suffocating its infant PC unit with a devastating return to old rules—the mainframe rules." By requiring a standardized software design, the company "killed any capacity within IBM to foster independent business models aimed at separate, unique computer industries."[5]

In the early '80s many companies in the United States became enamored with quality circles. Typically, these are groups of volunteers who meet for an hour every week to recommend ways to improve quality within their units. Companies reported significant benefits from these circles; then, in many places, they began to die. Activity Waned. People stopped attending; others came late. The recommendations became less significant. (In one organization, a quality circle argued over what radio station to play in the main work area.)

It would be easy to blame the people or the quality-circle process. But another view is to recognize that nothing lasts forever. These groups simply ran out of things they could do, given their limited mandate. Although the quality circles had been Integrated into the organization, it was time to let them go. One way to rejuvenate the cycle would be to expand the authority of the groups; another would be to move on to other forms of empowerment and quality improvement such as self-directed teams.

As much as we might want progress to be linear—one thing building on another in an inexorable rise toward perfection—it is most often cyclic. Today's award-winning idea can become tomorrow's joke. No stage lasts forever.

Each stage of the cycle has in it the seeds of its own destruction. For example, Implementation won't last forever. It will inevitably lead to Integration or failure. Waning Activity leads to either renewal or an ending. And on it goes.

# 3 MAKING MATTERS WORSE

Every great mistake has a halfway moment, a split second
when it can be recalled and perhaps remedied.
—*Pearl S. Buck*

D r. Seuss was wrong. Throughout his classic children's book
*Green Eggs and Ham,* Sam-I-Am pesters the main character until he finally relents and agrees to eat green eggs and
ham.[1] In real life, however, the Sam-I-Am approach doesn't
work so well. It usually increases resistance to your ideas.
Unfortunately, many corporate managers look to Sam-I-Am as a role model.

## OUR STRONG REACTION

Most people hate resistance. The mere mention of the word unleashes a torrent
of negative thoughts—fear, opposition, conflict, hassles, pain, annoyance,
anger, suspicion. Because it is viewed so negatively, people want to get over it. In
the words of so many articles on the subject, people want to *overcome* resis-

tance. This view is wrong. Attempts to overcome it usually make it worse. Here are just a few examples that I have noticed recently:

- A merger that never quite merged because little was done to listen to the concerns and ideas of those whose lives were going to be changed

- A new product that died even before it was born because the advocates tried to force its development before other departments had agreed to its merit

- A construction project that went way over budget because the various groups could not find ways to overcome their differences

- A quality improvement process that was never fully implemented because no one sought the support of the middle managers, who remained cynical about corporate leadership's commitment to the endeavor

- A large bank that annually spent hundreds of thousands of dollars for strategic plans that were never implemented because no one, except senior management and the consultants, cared about what was inside the handsomely bound tomes

Just a quick scan of the business press yields more examples. There is no shortage of failures attributable to poorly handled resistance.

Take the case of the D.C. football stadium. In the summer of 1992, Jack Kent Cooke, the owner of the Washington, D.C., football team, and Virginia Governor Douglas Wilder held a surprise press conference. They announced to a stunned audience that they were moving the team from the District of Columbia to Virginia. They showed precisely where the stadium would be located. They explained how the subway system would add a stop to handle game-day traffic. They showed a model of the proposed stadium. They seemed joyous and excited in their presentation.

Almost immediately, resistance began to develop. The people of Alexandria had other plans for the site. The subway authority didn't want to commit precious funds for a stop that would be used only eight times a year. The citizens of the state did not want to float a bond issue to support the project.

Cooke and Wilder reacted like many people in power: they ignored the resistance and forged ahead. Although nothing can be reduced to a single cause, I believe this was a major factor in the failure of their plans. As they pushed their idea, resistance increased in direct proportion to their actions, and within six months the project was dead.[2]

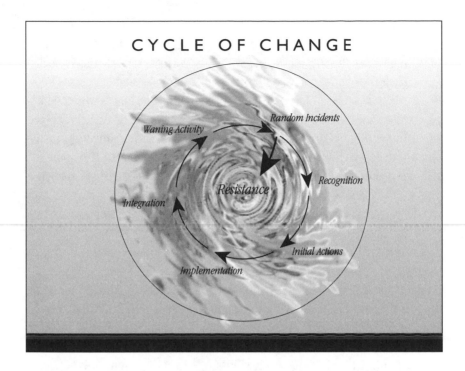

# CYCLE OF CHANGE

Random Incidents

Waning Activity

Resistance

Recognition

Integration

Initial Actions

Implementation

Examining this case in terms of the cycle, we can see that Cooke and Wilder were far out ahead of the people of Virginia (seven o'clock versus one o'clock). They expected, I am sure, that people would get on board and rapidly move around the cycle to join in support of this idea. It didn't happen. The harder Cooke and Wilder pushed ahead on the cycle, the deeper the Virginians' arrow turned inward and sank into resistance.

A few years ago, Du Pont attempted to open a new plant in Taiwan. Although Du Pont had worked in the country for years, this project failed because management failed to grasp the significance of a growing democracy. When local Taiwanese said they were concerned about environmental issues, Du Pont failed to listen, and the proposal died.[3]

In the next chapter you will see how Du Pont learned from this experience and later was able to build support for its plans for a new plant. And you'll read how a stadium got built in another city in spite of intense opposition.

## OUR DEFAULT POSITIONS

When we face resistance to our ideas, most of us react with an assortment of ineffective approaches. These are our default positions.[4] Unless we consciously make ourselves take some other action, when tensions run high, we revert to one of these default settings in dealing with others.

### Use Power

For many, the way to overcome resistance is to overpower it, to meet force with force. In this view, the only way to decrease opposition is to squelch those who disagree. Their use of power may be subtle: a gentle reminder that lets people know who the boss is; a joke during a meeting just so that no one forgets who conducts their performance reviews; a recollection of what happened to others who opposed similar initiatives. Or it may be blatant: ranting, raving, and striking fear into the hearts of those who dare go against their wishes. I am not suggesting that the use of power is always bad, but when it is used in an effort to *make* people support a change, it is seldom effective. When power is used on us, it drives our arrow down into the center faster than any other action. Unbridled power almost guarantees a tit-for-tat response: "Oh, yeah, let's just see you try to do that."

### Manipulate Those Who Oppose

Manipulation enjoys a long, rich history. In 1532, Niccolò Machiavelli wrote *The Prince,* a self-help manual for those aspiring to power. His advice on how to acquire and use power included ways to skillfully manipulate others—methods that are as effective today as they were half a millennium ago. We may conveniently fail to tell people the whole story until they have agreed to go along. We meet behind closed doors to determine ways to apply pressure on our opponents.

It is important to distinguish between the trickery described above and a more positive use of strategic thinking. For example, it makes perfect sense to determine who might be the best person to talk with staff about an upcoming change. Who has credibility? Whom will they listen to? Even though that decision might be made behind closed doors, the intent is to increase communication, not to trick people into complying.

### Apply Force of Reason

When we use force of reason, we try to overwhelm the other people with facts, figures, and flowcharts. This is the Sam-I-Am tactic. As you will see, giving people information can sometimes be a good way to deal with resistance, but this strategy is too much of a good thing. When we use force of reason, we turn up the volume way too high.

A manager asked for advice on how to build a bridge between his department and one down the hall—two departments that had long been enemies. Each side spoke badly about the other, and when they had to work together, each entered projects with reluctance and suspicion. People played their cards close to the vest.

My client's plan was to *tell* his counterpart all the reasons why he should want to build this bridge. I said, "Frank, it sounds to me like you want to *L.A. Law* them to death—give the jury such a barrage of facts that they can't help but throw up their hands and agree with you." Frank's intent (his name has been changed) was good; they *should* find ways to work cooperatively. But his *L.A. Law* style left no room for dialogue or for an exploration of why tensions ran so high between the units. Since in the past this approach had just added bricks to the wall, it was not likely to be any more successful this time.

### Ignore Resistance
Sometimes we view resistance like gnats at a picnic—a minor nuisance, but nothing to get concerned about. It seems that Cooke and Wilder ignored mounting resistance. After all, they were very powerful men, used to getting their way. How could little community groups possibly be a threat to an idea whose time had come?

Sometimes we ignore resistance simply because we want to believe that no one could seriously question our plans. We resist seeing the opposition mounting in front of us. We sometimes assume that, if we just keep moving forward, others will join in.

### Play Off Relationships
We use our friendship or common experience as a tool to get others to agree to our plan. They go along, not because it is such a good idea, but because they feel they owe it to us. This strategy often crumbles once people realize that our plan will cost them time or money—or runs counter to plans of their own.

If the change is minor, playing off relationships will probably work fine, but you are not reading this book to learn how to deal with insignificant change. It will be important to find ways to get others deeply interested in your ideas. To do this, you must engage them and be willing to be influenced by their ideas as well.

### Make Deals
Deal making is how the U.S. Congress works: I'll give you this, if you'll give me that. Deal making works fine if all we need is someone's vote. It can also work if resistance is low and the other people don't have a particular preference about the direction we intend to take. It does not work if resistance is high and if we need passion and commitment from people to support and implement the plan.

### Kill the Messenger
When the news is bad, instead of being thankful we get rid of the people who dare question us. Take this example from the Viet Nam War: "As the war effort began to fall apart in late 1962 and early 1963, the Military Assistance Command in Saigon set out to crush its own best officers in the field on behalf of its superiors in

Washington. . . . The Saigon commands systematically crushed all dissent from the field; the military channels did not brook dissent or negativism. If a colonel surfaced in a newspaper by name as a pessimist it was the end of his career."[5]

### Give In Too Soon

We may see the resistance as so strong that we give up before we ever know the true level of opposition or whether there might have been a way to arrive at some common understanding. I have seen middle managers so beaten down by the bureaucracy that they give up almost before they begin. They seem to live under a cloud of pessimism. As soon as the clouds begin to darken, they abandon their plans. They seldom wait to see how strong the storm will be.

Among these strategies you may recognize two or three of your personal default positions. Don't feel bad; these are the ways most of us deal with resistance. We anticipate what others might be thinking, and suddenly we find ourselves using a strategy without thinking about it.

It is important to consider your personal default positions as well as those your organization typically uses. For example, you may often use force of reason, while the corporation tends to use power without thinking. As we proceed, consider how you deal with resistance at both levels, the personal and the organizational. Understanding how you typically respond is the first step in finding better alternatives.

## WHY THE DEFAULT STRATEGIES DON'T WORK

The purpose of this book is to help you find ways to deal with resistance in order to build support for change. Given that goal, there are a number of reasons why these default approaches not only don't work but often escalate and strengthen opposition to your goals.

### They Increase Resistance

All of these approaches assume that your way is the right way and that others must be persuaded or forced to go along. Each is based on competition: someone will win, someone will lose.

When people feel they have something to lose, they fight back. The people of Taiwan didn't trust the giant American corporation. They were concerned about health and mobilized to stop a plant from being built in their city. When Cooke and Wilder ignored the opposition, the residents of northern Virginia formed groups to fight what they saw as a threat to their community.

We are a win-lose society. Every night, television serves up protagonists who win over their opponents. The sports pages tell us in banner headlines who won and who lost. News stories are framed as battles between adversaries, even when the contest seems to be only in the eye of the reporter.[6] This mind set can be so pervasive that we fail to even see that there might be other alternatives.

The problem with a win-lose mind set is that it limits our options when cooperation is called for. I like sports; I don't want baseball to change into a New Age event in which no one wins. But in the workplace, an us-versus-them model can be a killer. As our product design "team" tries to get a new product to market, we engage in a "full court press" to get it out the door before accounting can object. Headquarters "drives home" a new initiative. Our "home runs," "slam dunks," "two-minute drills," and "blitzes" make competitors of the people who should be our business partners.

Although we call this *healthy* competition, it is anything but. Assuming that our new idea will face stiff opposition, we begin to view the fight to save our dream as a battle royale. To the victor belong the spoils.

If competition is the only way, then it will be impossible to build alliances with all who have a stake in the outcome. Competition causes us to assume that our interests are at odds with those of other people, even though they may be sitting in the office next to ours.

### The Win Might Not Be Worth the Cost

In 279 B.C. the emperor Pyrrhus fought the Romans at Asculum. His army won, but at a tremendous cost in lives. He was said to have declared, "One more such victory and I am lost."[7] Such Pyrrhic victories are common in organizations.

Our desire to win at all costs blinds us to the toll it takes. In 1973, 20th Century Fox tried a new way of selling movies to television. Instead of selling rights for a fixed fee, they set up bidding wars between the networks. One of the first films offered was *The Poseidon Adventure*. The network executives couldn't stop themselves, even when they realized they had gone over their break-even point. It wasn't that they wanted the film so badly—they just didn't want another network to get it. ABC finally got the rights to show the film a single time for $3.3 million, knowing that they would probably lose over a million dollars![8]

ABC's "win" only cost them money. When competition this intense occurs inside an organization, your win can leave a bitter taste in the mouths of the losers. The Pyrrhic nature of the victory becomes evident when we try to build support for our next change. It is then we realize the cost of winning was too high.

Game theory teaches that in economics, trade, and even war, the unbridled urge to win escalates conflicts, often resulting in stalemates or extremely costly victories. Game theory searches for alternatives to these zero-sum games

## APPROACHES
## TO CHANGE AND RESISTANCE

### *Conventional*

**BELIEFS AND ASSUMPTIONS**

I believe change is linear. A leads to B, B leads to C.

I can plan and control all aspects of change.

I see change as a rational and objective process.

Emotional and personal issues should play no part in organizational change.

If it's my idea, it must be good (i.e., right, moral, sane, timely, non-fattening).

**TYPICAL BEHAVIORS**

Uses default strategies such as use of power, manipulation, and deal making in an attempt to influence or make people go along.

Avoids emotional and personal issues, so misses the message of resistance.

**PROBABLE RESULTS**

If support is needed for the change, there is a strong likelihood that it will fail (e.g., outright failure, significant cost or time overruns, a weak version of the original goal).

---

(games with a winner and a loser—or in this case, two losers) by suggesting that players look for strategies in which both sides can either win or keep losses to a minimum.[9]

### *They Fail to Create Synergy*
By showing an unwillingness to be influenced, we miss opportunities to hear information that could change our thinking. Those who resist may know something of the costs involved, the troubles that lie ahead, the possibilities or alternatives that we could never dream of.

### *They Create Fear and Suspicion*
When people lose, they have little reason to support us. For example, many organizations handle downsizing with little finesse, senior management typically using its power to announce its plans for the firings. Of course this ham-handed

## APPROACHES
## TO CHANGE AND RESISTANCE

### *Unconventional*

**BELIEFS AND ASSUMPTIONS**

Resistance is a natural part of any change.

The only effective way to deal with resistance is to invite and work with (rather than against) those who resist.

Change never ends. Today's support causes the seeds of tomorrow's dissatisfaction. And today's resistance carries the seeds of tomorrow's support.

**TYPICAL BEHAVIORS**

Engages others, finding ways to learn from those who resist and looking for ways to find common ground and join forces with them.

**PROBABLE RESULTS**

Builds excitement for the change.

Builds relationships and a foundation for future change.

Opportunity for creative solutions where most enjoy some benefit.

Keeps us from making decisions without full information.

approach causes great pain to those who are tossed out, but it also frightens those who remain. They wonder: Am I next? Just when its leaders believe they have made the organization lean and mean, they find that it is instead emaciated and weak.[10]

### *They Separate Us from Others*

Most important is the connection that must be developed and maintained between the person who wants the change and those whose support is needed. Instead of bringing us closer together, default strategies build walls between us, separating us even further. These strategies are audacious and arrogant. They say, in effect, that other people and their ideas are not worthy of our time or attention, or that their ideas are not as worthy as ours. On the other hand, when we use the default strategy of "Giving in too soon," our fear of losing keeps us from making any connection with others.

These common default-position approaches fail to listen to the voices of the people who resist. The implicit and extremely powerful message is that their fears, dreams, and ideas are unimportant. Yet most of us use these strategies repeatedly. We may seek to overpower others in ways subtle or flamboyant. We gently manipulate others into saying yes before they fully consider our ideas. Or we give up in anticipation of a protracted battle.

These strategies are so common, in fact, that we may find it difficult even to imagine that there might be another approach—one that's not just another variation on a competitive theme. Our experience may limit our ability to see these other possibilities. There is, however, another approach—an approach that is radically different.

# 4 SEEING THE POTENTIAL

> Always forgive your enemies—nothing annoys them so much.
> —*Oscar Wilde*

Resistance is not an impenetrable wall. Even though conventional approaches usually add bricks and mortar, there are reasonable and practical alternatives that increase our chances of getting beyond the barrier. Remember, these unconventional strategies are not mysterious; they just aren't used as often. Here are two stories that demonstrate how unconventional approaches can work.

## ANOTHER STADIUM

In April 1994 the Cleveland baseball team moved into their new home, Jacobs Field, in the heart of the city. The dream began in 1983 when some people in the community envisioned building a new, domed stadium so the team could move out of the cavernous old ball park on Lake Erie.

Resistance to the new stadium was high. Community groups argued that the city should instead spend money on housing and community services. Politicians were split over feasibility and cost. And some hardy souls simply preferred the old stadium with the wind whistling in off the lake.[1]

Many interests needed to converge for this project to be successful (and it almost died a number of times). The planners knew that they needed a strong base of support in order to proceed. They needed public approval for a bond issue as well as investment from the business community. Although deals were made and political pressure was put on some to go along, I believe the success of this project was due in large part to the way the planners found ways to transform resistance into support. In other words, they were willing to listen to those who opposed them.

For example, when they asked one influential community leader in northeast Ohio for his support, he refused. He didn't care much for baseball and didn't want money to go into a new stadium. Without his support, they would have had great difficulty getting many others to join in. Instead of reverting to a default approach such as manipulation or use of power, they kept on listening. He told them what he did care about—economic development for downtown Cleveland.

Keeping in mind their goal for a new stadium, they found ways to merge his goal into their vision. This was not a watered-down compromise, but collaboration, in the best sense. It was a solution that allowed both parties to meet their goals. Although they were unable to gain support from all parties who had a stake in it (even today, not everyone approves of the new stadium), they were able to earn the interest and support of enough individuals and groups to make Gateway a success.

Today the Gateway Center that houses Jacobs Field includes shops, restaurants, and a luxury hotel, and is the home of the basketball and hockey teams as well. This thriving complex may eventually revitalize downtown Cleveland. This is a significant improvement over the original vision, one that simply would have transferred the team from one location to another without much long-term financial benefit to the city.

## LEARNING FROM EXPERIENCE

In 1989, two years after failing to get permission to build a titanium oxide plant in Kuan Yin, Taiwan, Du Pont tried again.

Democracy had been growing in the country, and people now demanded to be included. Due to a strong economy, citizens began paying closer attention to quality-of-life issues such as environmental pollution. Even though the company had been building plants in the country for fifty years, conditions had changed, and Du Pont had to do things differently.

One of the company's biggest plants, near the proposed site, had enjoyed good employee relations. Du Pont asked its employees to speak with family and friends in the neighboring town, giving them time off for these meetings. In addition, Du Pont arranged bus trips to the plant to give residents an opportunity to see the operation and talk informally with employees.

The community was notified of environmental impact meetings, and Du Pont worked with leaders of the township as they developed their plan. The debate was hot at times, but most important, there was a debate. Du Pont learned that the proposed site housed temples and burial grounds; the company suggested building two fences around the facility, one to secure the plant and the other to give people access to the sacred sites. The company placed a trailer near the site so that residents of the area could stop in at any time and talk with a Du Pont representative about the proposals.

It took some eighteen months to build enough support to get the new plant approved, but construction began in 1991. Today, the plant is operating and, with no environmental problems to date, support continues to grow.[2]

## WHY THE UNCONVENTIONAL WORKED

The Cleveland planners and Du Pont succeeded because they avoided or minimized the use of the default approaches.

### They Took Resistance Seriously

Both enterprises recognized the potential power of resistance; they had experienced it before. They knew they had no choice but to deal with the opposition; ignoring it would not be an option. When resistance is worthy of the name, it does not go away on its own. It must be tended to.

### They Treated Those Who Resisted with Respect

The Cleveland planners had the sense to hear the answer to, "What do you care about?" They met with many community groups to listen to concerns and search for ways to bring others into the process. In Taiwan, the debates were out in the open, giving people an opportunity to speak and to listen.

### They Designed Structures That Aided Communication

Du Pont was savvy in the way it communicated. The company understood that its employees were its greatest allies. Who better, in an Asian country that places great emphasis on family and the wisdom of age, to discuss concerns with the people of Kuan Yin? In addition, setting up the information trailer made it easy for townspeople to learn about the company's plans.

### *They Took the Long View*

Baseball stadiums and chemical plants, like ancient Rome, are not built in a day. A more forceful approach, one that pushed the cycle quickly in the interest of saving time, would probably have killed both projects.

I find it interesting how hard it is to grasp this concept. Clients often agree with me that they must build support for their ideas, then, in the same breath, say they don't have time for that right now. They want to push ahead, even when their experience tells them they are likely to fail.

Our own resistance to taking the time to engage resistance is a major reason for failure. We believe that getting others involved will slow us down too much. Indeed, that can happen. But by moving more cautiously we have an opportunity to build commitment from the people who must approve or implement our dream.

Some of the models for large organizational change now gaining in popularity stand traditional planning on its head. They go fast and deep. By bringing together all who have a stake to wrestle with issues of common concern, they create a common strategy.

### *They Sought Mutual Gain*

Both organizations were influenced by those who resisted. Cleveland expanded its vision from a simple stadium to a multiuse complex; Du Pont found ways to honor the traditions of the people in the area.

The unifying theme here is to blend cycles, not just get others to join the parade. The Cleveland planners made a significant shift when they began talking about economic development. The discussion evolved from a construction project to a vision of potentially greater benefits for the city. This expanded goal allowed others to get excited about the project because it addressed their interests as well. The new vision allowed a convergence of many cycles.

I am not suggesting that these unconventional strategies were the only actions Du Pont and the Cleveland planners used. I have yet to find individuals or groups who avoid default positions entirely. However, the point should be clear that both groups took deliberate and prolonged actions that built support for their ideas by engaging the needs and wishes of those who opposed them.

## A CONTRAST IN STYLES

A significant difference between default and less conventional strategies lies in how we view the world. The default approaches tend to be linear: if I do A, then B will happen. It is difficult to avoid this cause-and-effect thinking; it's part of how we view the world.

The default positions might be viewed as a menu of linear A-causes-B options. Whether use of power, manipulation, or killing the messenger, these strategies attempt to get someone else to do something. We believe that these actions will result in the desired behavior. When the strategy fails, we assume that we have simply chosen the wrong one, and so we pick another from the list. In choosing from this faulty menu, we fail to realize that the options all stem from the same belief that we can make people do our bidding.

Conventional or default strategies are predicated on the belief that we can control everything, that our actions will lead to intended consequences—in other words, that good planning leads inevitably to good results. That's a nice fantasy, but it seldom works. People don't respond like Pavlov's dogs, salivating when we ring the bell. Novelist Philip Roth suggests a Rule of Twenty-six.[3] For every action we take, there are twenty-six unintended consequences—some good, some bad, but all unpredictable. I think he's right. We can neither control nor predict the actions others will take.

If the Cleveland planners had relied on the default tactics too often, they might have created opposition in many unforeseen ways; consider the Washington fiasco. Du Pont learned its lesson in Taiwan and applied a very different set of strategies in its successful bid to gain support for its new plant.

I don't believe that most of us truly want to force others to do our bidding, but our world view may make it difficult to see other options. Couple that linear A-causes-B mind set with the time pressures most of us face, and we are left feeling that we have no choice but to bulldoze the wall that stands in front of us.

## ENTER THE UNKNOWN

Dealing with resistance can be chaotic. When we ask another group, "What do you care about?" we cannot predict the response or the ways in which we might be able to blend efforts to work toward a more mutually satisfying goal. We can't guarantee that their wishes will align with ours at all. Out of fear of what we will hear, we play it safe and don't ask.

We can engage resistance in the belief that we will get through it, but we can't be certain what it will look like on the other side. Entering resistance is like buying a ticket to a carnival fun house designed by Ray Bradbury. Its world is distorted. We feel out of place and not quite sure what awaits us. The fun house is both frightening and exhilarating. Having walked through Bradbury's off-kilter world, we emerge from it changed in some fundamental way. Our view of the same old dusty fairgrounds is forever altered. When we fully engage with those who resist us, our views do change. Something shifts. We leave the carnival different from when we entered.[4]

## TWO FUNDAMENTAL QUESTIONS

Two questions should guide our exploration of resistance. The first is usually fairly easy to answer; the second is more difficult.

### *What's in It for Me?*

We know why we are excited about the proposed change. The Cleveland planners could see the benefits of having a newer stadium designed just for baseball. Since Du Pont knew Taiwan had a good business climate, they could see the benefits of the new plant.

But if we consider only the first question we will be tempted to rely on the default positions. If meeting our own goals is the only important thing, then our strategies are likely to reflect that self-centered bias. We must ask the second question as well.

Language has a subtle, yet powerful effect on the way we view the world. English, like most other Western languages, is linear—its basic sentence construction, noun-verb-noun, translates into a world view of 'x causes y.' This linear view predisposes us to focus on one-way relationships rather than on circular or mutually causative ones, where x influences y, and y in turn influences x. Unfortunately, many of the most vexing problems confronting managers and corporations today are caused by a web of tightly interconnected circular relationships.[5]

—*Michael Goodman*
"*Systems Thinking As Language*"

### *What's in It for Them?*

This second question is seldom asked. We are often so blinded by our own brilliant idea that we fail to consider that the other people may have wants, needs, ideas, and fears that differ from ours. This oversight encourages resistance. Our idea comes in conflict with theirs. Many who lived in northern Virginia had other plans for the stadium site. Still others saw a football arena as an affront to a rather agreeable status quo. The problem was not that there wasn't something in it for the Virginians, it was that no one considered how to blend the interests of the stadium promoters with the interests of the people who lived near the site. In contrast, the Cleveland planners were able to merge the goal of economic development with the dream of a new stadium.

When we do consider the "What's in it for them?" question, we often limit our thinking to answers influenced by our own point of view. We color our response by stating things the way we would like others to think. "If they knew what was good for them, they'd see that this restructuring is the best thing for the company." "If she'd just wake up and smell the coffee, she'd realize that her department has got to cut budget by 20 percent." "Those poor people should realize that a new stadium would be the best thing to hit this town in years." These answers reflect only our view of what is needed. They are simply slick reworkings of the "What's in it for me?" question.

People seldom say, "If I really cared about this company, I'd go along with your restructuring plan. But my role in life is to obstruct and to make things miserable for those who want to get things done." Most people don't think that way. Our failure to seriously consider the second question means that we will always see those who resist as adversaries. We are doomed to view them as those people with tiny brains who salivate at the thought of destroying our dreams. And if we hold that negative view of them, we are not likely to want to work *with* them to create something new.

## A THIRD QUESTION

Be careful when addressing the "What's in it for them?" question. As a starting point it is a good question, but it should be replaced quickly with "What's in it for us?" As one representative from Du Pont said, they had to "walk in their shoes, drink their tea, sit in their tea stalls" or else they would miss learning what was in it for them. Once we begin to learn about the concerns and dreams of others, we often find our thinking shifting to "What's in it for us?"

## WHY BOTHER?

There are several good reasons to bother with this unconventional approach.

### We Can Learn Something

Often those who resist have something

**B**arbara Tuchman writes that the causes of folly are quite simple, "a factor usually overlooked by political scientists who, in discussing the nature of power, always treat it, even when negatively, with immense respect. They fail to see it as sometimes a matter of ordinary men walking into water over their heads, acting unwisely or foolishly or perversely as people in ordinary circumstances frequently do. The trappings and impact of power deceive us, endowing the possessors with a quality larger than life. Shorn of his tremendous curled peruke, high heels, and ermine, the Sun King was a man subject to misjudgment, error and impulse—like you and me."[6]

important to tell us. We can be influenced by them. People resist for what they view as good reasons. They may see alternatives we never dreamed of. They may understand problems about the minutiae of implementation that we could never see from our lofty perch high atop Mount Olympus. If the planners had failed to hear the strong voice of resistance in Cleveland there would be no Gateway Complex.

Sometimes we need to hear the resistance in order to know that our plans are doomed to failure. In *The March of Folly,* Barbara Tuchman describes many situa-

## NATURAL CHANGE

### AN INTERVIEW WITH MARGARET WHEATLEY

*Margaret Wheatley is the author of the best-selling* Leadership and the New Science, *an exploration of the ways in which the discoveries in sub-atomic physics and chaos theory might be applied in organizations. Since resistance is a part of the natural world, it seemed that her thinking might help illuminate the conversation on the subject.*

**RM:** You've written that the Newtonian mechanistic model hinders our ability to change.

**MW:** It is an absolute mental block created by our machine images. Machines only change within very narrow limits. I think that we don't understand at all how well equipped we are as living organisms to deal with change in a creative way, so that resistance becomes a much different issue—minimized in some ways. I absolutely believe that the whole focus on resistance to change is just a by-product of very bad change processes. The resistance we are experiencing in organizations says nothing about human nature or our innate ability to deal with change in a changing world.

**RM:** What is resistance in your view?

**MW:** Resistance is people's assertion of their identity as they presently construct it.

**RM:** So if current change processes threaten that identity, how should we view change?

**MW:** The world is self-organizing. Everywhere we look, we see change going on—change,

tions in which leaders failed to read obvious warning signs. In 1685, for instance, Louis XIV rescinded the Edict of Nantes that had provided safety for the Protestant Huguenots, thus opening the door to their persecution. The country praised this action. Even at Louis XIV's death, this was cited as one of his most praiseworthy acts. In what may have been the only dissent, the Dauphin, the king's chief advisor, warned the king that revoking the edict might cause mass emigrations and harm to commerce. The king didn't listen, but, to his credit, didn't behead his advisor either.

The results were devastating. Thousands of skilled workers fled the country, depopulating many regions. Other European nations welcomed the Huguenots with open arms and enticing tax incentives. A Protestant coalition against France was strengthened in Europe. In France, the Protestants who remained redoubled growth and development, and increasing complexity. All of these things are evident everywhere and they are evident in our own lives. Then we get into organizations in which change becomes not an ability, but just a huge problem for us. I think we need to stop looking at human nature negatively and look at our change processes with much more discernment. We do have a self-organizing capacity in us, which means that we will change in order to maintain ourselves. Change is not foreign. In the natural world change is not a singular event you try to live through, it's just the way things are. I think the saying "People don't resist change, they resist being changed" sums it up.

**RM:** What are the implications if people don't resist change itself, but only resist being changed?

**MW:** A person in one organization said resistance to change is like a mantra we feed ourselves: "In every team meeting we get together and spend the first twenty minutes saying change is hard. People resist change." This is an unexamined belief about human nature. Our assumptions about stability and the promises of equilibrium were all false promises and that is not how life is. If people participate from the beginning of the change they are able to re-identify or change their identity so that it doesn't feel threatening.

their faith, causing an even wider split between the two Christian groups. The revocation raised questions about investing monarchs with absolute power. (Three generations later the monarchy was overthrown in the French Revolution.)

In all the examples Tuchman notes, the warnings were not only clear but repeated. It's our failure to listen over an extended period that gets us into trouble.

### *Giving Others a Voice May Dissipate Resistance*
Being heard is powerful. It can unleash energy. When we believe that others really care to hear our stories, we begin to build a bond with them. Truly listening and seeking to find that common ground is the polar opposite of the default strategies, in which getting our own way reigns supreme.

As David Bohm has written, dialogue is a way of finding common meaning through words.[7] Unlike discussion, in which we toss ideas back and forth, dialogue slows conversations down to discover the assumptions and values and world views of those who face us. The object of dialogue is to learn, not to convince. During dialogue we often find common threads running deep beneath the surface.

In Utah there is a three-hundred-acre forest of aspen called the Pando Clone. On the surface it looks like thousands of separate trees, but scientists digging down into the root system have found that all the trees came from a single seedling, and that many still share a common root system. Quite often, through open dialogue, as we learn why people hold particular views, we begin to see that their hopes and fears are either highly compatible or strikingly similar to ours. Only by listening can we hope to find that common root.

Forestry researchers can easily spot the signs of a common genosystem. They examine for bark thickness, leaf formation, branching, and so forth. As we gain skills in listening to the concerns of others, we can begin to spot similar common patterns that show us that we are often far more similar than superficial appearances might lead us to believe.

Even if we don't find a common base, at least we have learned where we stand. We are far better informed, better able to make decisions. Even if we find that resistance is so deeply embedded that to continue would be folly, think of the savings in blood, sweat, and tears—not to mention time and money.

### It Keeps Us on Track

According to the research of Everett Rogers on how innovations get accepted or rejected, the people who promote a new idea—the change agents—tend to see primarily the positive aspects and to minimize the risks. For example, when missionaries introduced the steel axe to an Australian aboriginal tribe,

> the change agents intended that the new tool should raise levels of living and material comfort for the tribe. But the new technology also led to the breakdown of the family structure, the rise of prostitution, and "misuse" of the innovation itself. . . . Seldom are the change agents able to predict another aspect of an innovation's consequences, its meaning, the subjective perception of the innovation by the clients.[8]

We must change our thinking. We must find better ways to articulate the answers to "What's in it for me?" and far better ways of finding the answers to "What's in it for them?"

# 5 GETTING BEYOND THE WALL

You philosophers are lucky men. You write on paper, and paper is patient. Unfortunately, Empress that I am, I write on the susceptible skins of living beings.
—*Catherine the Great*

Since dealing with strong resistance is difficult, we sometimes allow our worst fears to take over. In the classic comedy movie *Duck Soup*, Rufus T. Firefly (Groucho Marx), leader of Freedonia, waits for the arrival of the ambassador from the neighboring country of Sylvania. The ambassador's apology, and Firefly's acceptance, would avoid a war that neither side can afford. But as Groucho waits, his thoughts run riot.

I'd be unworthy of the high trust that's been placed in me if I didn't do everything in my power to keep our beloved Freedonia at peace with the world. I'd be only too happy to meet Ambassador Trentino and offer him, on behalf of my country, the right hand of good fellowship. And, I feel sure he will accept this gesture in the spirit with which it is offered. But suppose he doesn't? A fine thing that'll be.

I hold out my hand and he refuses to accept it. That'll add a lot to my prestige, won't it? Me, the head of a country, snubbed by a foreign ambassador. Who does he think he is, that he can come here and make a sport out of me in front of all my people? Think of it, I hold out my hand and that hyena refuses to accept it. Why, the cheap, four-flushing swine. He'll never get away with it, I tell you, he'll never get away with it. [Trentino enters ready to make peace.] So, you refuse to shake hands with me, huh? [Groucho slaps him and the war begins.][1]

Granted, Marx Brothers' films aren't real life, but how often have we been swept away by our own fantasies? Instead of engaging the other people in a constructive manner, we allow our worst fears to take over. As we look at the formidable wall of resistance standing in front of us, it's easy to rely on default tactics in an attempt to get past it or destroy it quickly. Touchstones can help.

Touchstones were once used to test the purity of gold and silver by rubbing metal against them. If the metal left a certain streak, it was pure. The touchstones in this book work in the same way. As we consider strategies, touchstones can let us know if they pass the test. I have identified five fundamental touchstones that can keep us from emulating Groucho:

- Maintain Clear Focus
- Embrace Resistance
- Respect Those Who Resist
- Relax
- Join with the Resistance

The touchstones provide a reference point. We may ignore one or two of them without harm, but if our plans run counter to any of them, then we must rethink the strategy or risk failure.

But don't take my word for their value; test them. Compare times when you have successfully built support for change with those times when everything you did seemed to increase opposition. Look at changes around you and ask, Why did one succeed and the other fail?

## TOUCHSTONE NO. 1: MAINTAIN CLEAR FOCUS

When facing resistance, it's easy to lose your way. Clear Focus is like a beacon in the fog. Even when everything is covered in a deep mist, the beacon keeps you on course. As the fog of resistance thickens, it's easy to lose sight of your objective. When people attack your ideas, you may forget your original goal of building support for the change, and replace it with a new one—getting even. Keeping your goal in mind can help you stay on course while navigating through dangerous shoals.

### Keep Both Long and Short View

The civil rights movement adopted an old labor song, "Keep Your Eyes on the Prize," as its anthem. It reminded people that the journey would be a long one and that it was important to keep their sights on the long-range goal, the prize of justice and equality. The perils of the civil rights movement were so high that it would have been easy to lose focus, to lash out at those who sought to keep people down. That song and speeches like "I Have a Dream" helped people keep their sights on the distant goal and not treat each injustice as a major loss. Without the guiding focus, it would have been extremely difficult for people to stick with nonviolence and keep subjecting themselves to physical and mental abuse.

You must maintain a dual focus: one eye on the goal and the other on the work of the moment. Some people who wear contact lenses have one lens focused far and the other near. By shifting their eyes, they can see equally well at close range and at a distance. You must be able to do the same when you work with those who resist you. When you Maintain Clear Focus you can shift your sight back and forth between what is happening in front of you at the moment and still keep your eyes on the distant prize.[2]

### Persevere

When resistance is strong, your focus must include perseverance. Major changes often require incredible stamina. In 1959, nine years after the Chinese invasion of Tibet, Tibetan Buddhists escaped to India, where the Dalai Lama, their spiritual leader, set up headquarters in exile. The Buddhists remain there today, unable to return to their homeland. On a visit to the United States in 1994, the Dalai Lama was asked, "Of all your teachers, who was the greatest?" His response: Chairman Mao. It was Mao, he said, who taught him patience.

Focus turned to perseverance keeps you from turning back when the going gets tough. Robert Frey, owner and president of Cinmade, a small manufacturer of composite cans in Cincinnati, envisioned a place that "allows people at all levels of the company to make decisions as if they owned the company." He wanted to change the traditional management–employee relationship that bred mistrust and to introduce profit sharing as a way to make everyone a partner in the business. He wanted hourly staff to hire the plant manager and have veto power over all hiring decisions.

Resistance was extremely high. Workers distrusted what they saw as a management ploy. Why would a successful businessman want to change? It didn't make sense. Their union thought this was a union-busting tactic.

It took four years before people saw that he was serious and started coming around. He opened the books and gave people a monthly state-of-the-business report. Throughout, he kept his eyes on his prize and persevered with his goal of making the company an exemplary workplace. Today, Cinmade is a model of management–labor cooperation.[3]

## TOUCHSTONE NO. 2: EMBRACE RESISTANCE

To get beyond the wall, you must explore and Embrace Resistance. To do this, you must let down your guard and enter the world of those who resist you.

Embracing Resistance is counterintuitive. It goes against your natural instincts of protecting yourself and staying out of harm's way. Those who have run rapids in rafts, kayaks, or canoes know that when their craft is headed broadside toward a large rock, the best move is to lean downstream, toward the rock. Leaning into the rock exposes more of the bottom of the boat to the downstream current, giving you time to maneuver. Leaning away from the rock tilts you upstream, allowing the current to catch the edge of the boat and flip it over.

Far too many times I have disregarded what I've known to be true and found myself swimming through white water. My training and experience told me what I should do, but when I saw a massive boulder approaching, my instincts shouted, "Get away from that rock, Maurer, you're going to get hurt." Even today, I must remind myself repeatedly to lean downstream or else my powerful—and wrong—instincts will take over.

Embracing Resistance requires the same counterintuitive response. You must move toward the resistance or risk being capsized.

### *Why Move Toward Resistance?*

If your goal is to build commitment for your ideas, you must know what blocks it. Who opposes you? What is their opposition to this idea? Do they hate the idea itself? The way you plan to implement? Is there an ageless animosity toward your group? Is it something personal directed toward you? Without exploring the resistance, you can only guess. If you guess wrong you may have to pay a price later—the price of even deeper resistance.

The voice of resistance tells you what's wrong. Once you know why people are concerned, you can attempt to find common ground.

Salespeople know that getting prospective customers to state their objections unlocks possibilities. Once they know the objections, they can respond. Sometimes the response can be as simple as providing more information, such as working out another way of financing the deal. If the resistance to buying is deeper, the sales-person has an opportunity at least to try to address those concerns. Salespeople know that they cannot close many sales without identifying and working through the objections. They do not avoid the opposition, they invite it. They understand that energy is embedded in that resistance, and the only way to transform it is to understand it. Although salespeople could use this new information to manipulate and mislead, they can also use it to merge both interests: solving a client's problem and making a sale.

Embracing Resistance demands that you hear the reasons beneath the reasons—the things those who resist say to each other when you are not around. These are things that you must find ways to hear.

## TOUCHSTONE NO. 3:
## RESPECT THOSE
## WHO RESIST

**T**he human brain is, in large part, a machine for winning arguments, a machine for convincing others that its owner is in the right—and thus a machine for convincing the owner of the same thing. The brain is like a good lawyer: given any set of interests to defend, it sets about convincing the world of their moral and logical worth, regardless of whether they in fact have any of either.[5]
—*Robert Wright*
   The Moral Animal

Some managers in a Fortune 500 financial services company have adopted one of their company's operating principles: Assume positive motivation. People who work there have told me that remembering that principle has changed the way they interact with others: they assume the other person is acting honorably until proven wrong. You give up nothing by treating people with Respect. Although there are never guarantees, this approach is the only way you can ever hope to build trust.

Think about your colleagues. Some of them seem to invite conflict and antagonism wherever they go; everything is a battle. Others seem to have a gift for respecting people. Tony Snow, reporter for the *Detroit Free Press,* in a remembrance of syndicated columnist Hobart Rowan, recalled how much he enjoyed debating Rowan. Even though they were often on opposite sides of an issue, Rowan was always civil and seemed genuinely interested in hearing other points of view.

> He was also somebody who agreed to disagree with people amicably. And, in this age of all or nothing politics, it's always refreshing to have a colleague—with whom you disagree—to do it [with] and you end up thinking better of them after the argument because you learn something from what they have to say and you simply enjoyed the conversation.[4]

### The Struggle for Respect
You will seldom have difficulty describing "What's in it for me?" You know why the

change is needed and what the benefits and risks are to you. The more you think about the change, the stronger grows your belief that your way is the right way.

When you feel strongly about an idea, it is hard to imagine any other point of view. When people suggest another idea or simply state that they won't support your proposal, you tend to ascribe motives to them. They are out to get you. They aren't as bright as you are. They don't care. They are selfish, and out for the wrong number one.

Like Groucho, as you magnify your invented thoughts, you tend to view those who resist as people not worthy of your respect. Once you cover them with this shroud, your ability to listen ends. You no longer have any hope of learning the answer to the question "What's in it for them?"

### Respect vs. Trust

There may be times when you don't trust others, but that doesn't mean that you should treat them with disrespect. It is important not to confuse trust or fondness with Respect. Respect is a behavior, not a belief. Opponents shake hands before a game as a sign of Respect and a way of acknowledging the other person, not necessarily to indicate that they will go dancing later. Civil rights leaders would have been fully justified in acting with rage in response to the indignities heaped on African Americans by those who oppressed them, yet I can think of no public action by the late Martin Luther King that was anything less than dignified.

### Listen with Interest

Showing respect requires that you listen deeply with an open heart and mind. You must be interested in them and the stories they tell you. Organizational consultant Edwin Nevis suggests that you need to be like Columbo.[6] Police detective Columbo always seemed genuinely curious about the people he questioned; he was interested in hearing what they had to say and learning more about them; he had a capacity to temporarily suspend judgment and allow his curiosity to take over. You don't need to agree with others, but you do need to understand them.

Listen to your silent reactions to the prospect of talking with people who disagree with you. If you hear an internal voice warning you to watch your backside, or feel yourself rolling your eyes when their names are mentioned, or find yourself joking about them before meeting them, you need to watch out. Of course you will feel what you feel, but you must at least find ways to treat them with Respect.

### Tell the Truth

I have seen resistance melt for no other reason than that the person responsible for the change continually told people the truth. A plant manager received applause from all his employees on the day he closed their plant. Although the closing would leave many without jobs and little prospect of finding similar employment, they were showing their appreciation for the way he handled the change: he told the truth.

## TOUCHSTONE NO. 4: RELAX

Dealing with resistance can be very stressful. People attack you and your precious ideas. Sometimes they seem to show no Respect for you. Relaxation is key; the more you Relax, the easier it will be for you to Embrace Resistance.

Ask someone to push against your hands. Your natural inclination is to push back; it is very difficult to stop that automatic response. Only by Relaxing can you deactivate the default reaction and move with the force coming at you.[7]

In the ancient Chinese martial art of T'ai Chi, opponents spar by pushing hands. As one pushes, the other pulls back. If your opponent pushes to your left, you yield, giving nothing to resist. As you push, he yields. Each push demands that you be perfectly Relaxed and able to move with the force pushing against you. The winner is seldom the stronger person, but the one who is able to stay relaxed longer. When an opponent tenses, he is unable to yield to the push and can be toppled with little effort.

There is little in our culture that is analogous to this gentle and powerful form of boxing; our idea of dealing with resistance comes from the Arnold Schwarzenegger school. Even when you try to slow down and listen, your internal Terminator awaits a chance to blow them away. This win-at-all-costs mind set may work fine when you are engaged in a contest such as tennis. But it doesn't work when you are trying to build alliances.

### Stay Calm to Stay Engaged

Relaxing does not mean giving in or giving up. It simply means staying calm to stay engaged. As the other person attacks your position, you listen, you draw her out. In short, you invite her push. Once she has pushed, once she has said it all, you are still standing. You have done nothing to alienate her. You have not given away the ranch. You have simply listened.

Once the other person has pushed, you have options. You can counterattack, of course, but you're not likely to build support that way. Or you can use what you've just learned as a way to begin seeking a common ground. This second, unconventional, option is not possible if you are tense.

### Know Their Intentions

By Relaxing while you Embrace Resistance, you can learn what causes others to resist. Tension limits your ability to see the full picture. As William Reed, an Aikido master, reminds us, "When gripped by anger or fear, the range of peripheral vision becomes narrowly focused on a point. In extreme cases it may shut out everything but the opponent's face or weapon."[8] Relaxed, you can learn to anticipate their intention, or at least pick up on more subtle cues. The more you know about their hopes and fears, the actions they might take, the more options you have.

The more Relaxed you are, the more you can be in control. You can lead with calm confidence. Just before battle, the Samurai warriors of Japan often practiced the tea ceremony, an ancient ritual that quiets the mind.[9] Unlike American athletes with their butt-slapping bonhomie, these fearsome warriors believed that they were at their best when at their quietest.

We most often think of Relaxation as limited to the individual, but organizations need to consider ways to Relax as well. Clear ground rules, for instance, can help all parties Relax knowing that a meeting will not become a blood bath.

## TOUCHSTONE NO. 5: JOIN WITH THE RESISTANCE

Building support for change comes from blending your intentions with theirs. The secret is in finding ways to combine the answers to "What's in it for me?" and "What's in it for them?"

As you explore the resistance, you begin to listen for common fears and common interests. You listen for ways to join cycles in a common vision. Although your goals may differ, the solution should attempt to capture the concerns of all parties.

### Begin Together

If you are at the beginning of the change, you have the possibility of joining with the resistance to create something new. Before opinions have had time to calcify, you can search for a common vision. Put in terms of the cycle, if everyone is somewhere near Random Incidents and Recognition, then together you can create a common understanding of the issues and develop a plan jointly.

### Change the Game

Another way to Join is to change the rules right from the beginning, so that there is nothing to resist. When singer John Denver began playing large arenas, he wanted to keep the homey, personal flavor of smaller concerts. He envisioned playing in the round on a low stage, with the audience seated only three feet away. This is not how it is usually done. At a typical concert for this age group, a phalanx of uniformed guards separates the audience from the performers.

Denver and his friend Tom Crum came up with another approach. They met with security personnel before concerts and included them in their planning. They asked the staff to act as ushers and take seats near the aisles during the show. They never had a problem. However, whenever they experimented with posting only a few guards at the corners of the stage, people would invariably try to get on stage. Once they were on stage, it was difficult to get them off.[10] It was the implied barriers between Denver and the audience that created the challenge. When there was nothing to push against, people didn't push.

This approach was in the spirit of rising above the limitations of zero-sum games. When you change the game, you move toward one in which all can gain. But this is extremely difficult. How can you be sure they won't rush the stage? You'd better be safe and post a few guards. Then people rush the stage, confirming your self-fulfilling prophecy. It's that deadly loop that keeps us from rising above the zero-sum game.

### Find Themes and Possibilities

If you are embroiled in a debate that is bitterly polarized, then you must listen beyond the rhetoric to try to find ways to join others. Consider the longstanding antagonism between the rice growers of the Sacramento Valley and those who want to preserve its scarce wetlands. Once, 45 million birds wintered there, and now estimates put the number closer to 10 percent of that figure. Rice growers need water—lots of water. Approximately 40 percent of the state's water goes to agriculture. Migratory birds need considerable amounts of water as well. Each year farmers flood their fields, then drain them once the harvest is in, leaving them dry for the winter. Author Mark Reisner called it "the monsoon crop of the desert."[11]

The situation seemed bleak. It was a war of farmers against hunters and environmentalists. But things are changing. Ducks Unlimited, the Nature Conservancy, and the rice industry have found a way to join in common cause.

Some farmers reflood their fields after harvest. This provides habitat for migrating birds—and the migrating birds tamp down the rice stalks and provide free natural fertilizer. It also replaces the usual practice of burning the three tons per acre of "rice straw," which fills the valley with smoke and adds to California's air pollution. (Burning will be banned in the year 2000.)

Doug McGagen, manager of Gunnersfield Ranch and now the chairman of the Ricelands Habitat Partnership, said, "My resistance was to moving, you know, away from cultural practices we were used to. Any time you've done a certain thing a certain way, such as putting your pants on your right leg first and then your left leg, if somebody tells you you're gonna have to do it the opposite way, you know, it's just gonna feel pretty uncomfortable for a while."

This success in the Sacramento Valley did not come easily. Resistance to working together was deep and the interests seemed far apart. It was only when the parties got beyond the stereotypes and assumptions and began to consider what oth-

## TAKING THEIR SIDE
### AN INTERVIEW WITH PETER BLOCK

*Peter Block is the author of many best-selling management books* (Flawless Consulting, The Empowered Manager, *and* Stewardship) *and a highly regarded organizational consultant. He has a unique ability to state clearly what others wish they had said. I have long admired his thinking on the subject of resistance.*

**RM:** Peter, how do you handle resistance?

**PB:** I don't believe that resistance is a problem or something to be overcome, so part of how I handle it is how I think about it. We rarely experience our own resistance—so we don't want somebody to overcome it. All the combative language about resistance only intensifies it: If we overcome it, get around it, reduce it, deal with it—all those verbs indicate that it is a problem to be solved. Resistance is simply a reluctance to choose.

We have just not made up our mind whether to yield and surrender to what's asked of us or to keep on as is. Our inability to choose is an emotional issue usually stuck on questions like: What's the point? How optimistic am I about the future and what it holds? How vulnerable do I feel at this moment?

**RM:** What do you do when you face people who resist you?

**PB:** I say, "How can I take their side?" They must be acting with good cause, with good reason, so I support the resistance. I support people not making a choice—I can also live with whatever choice they make. The problem occurs when I have a stake in their actions. Then I need to ask myself, "Why is that a problem? Who am I to say what

ers might want, that alternatives became apparent. Their partnership rose above a zero-sum game in which one's goal is in direct opposition to the opponent. Rather than working on separate cycles, each with its own goals and strategies, they found ways to join interests.

### THE FLIP SIDE
Everything has another side, and so do the touchstones.[12] As good as they are, they can be misused or taken too far. (However, it is far more common for them to be

**they** ought to be doing? Who is to say that I am the enlightened one?"

**RM:** How do you support a client's resistance?

**PB:** I exaggerate. I love the edge. If people are fearful, I reframe their fear in life and death terms. If people are having trouble influencing others, I say "What if there is no way in the world they will ever go along with you?" Somehow in the extreme people can let go of their caution, their judgment, their ambivalence. I think extreme language dramatizes choice. And I make light of what first seems heavy. I might say, "So, what's the problem? You're going to die anyway. Why don't you just decide what position you want to be in when it happens?"

**RM:** You've said that you love the phrase "what you see is what you get." How come?

**PB:** It makes me responsible for the universe and it puts my life back in my hands. It forces me to question my view of events and gives me an enormous amount of choice over how I experience the world. I like this idea. Someday I hope to experience it.

**RM:** Any words for those people who think all this is garbage and want to overcome resistance?

**PB:** I'd say, "Do you want to win or do you want to work things out? Maybe you're reading the wrong book. Maybe you should read *You Are What You Eat*."

underused.) Maintain Clear Focus can turn into a locked position if you are not careful. Focus means simply to keep your sights on the vision, knowing that you will probably be influenced by others along the way. If you forget to engage others, then your focus turns to "Win at all costs."

"Embrace Resistance" is the overarching theme of this book, but it is possible to take this theme too far. You can get carried away with the reactions and lose yourself inside the resistance. By doing so, you lose all sight of reality and miss opportunities to move ahead.

If you lose your Clear Focus and apply only Respect, you run the risk of giving in to others, so that they get their way and you get nothing—no passion, no fire. It is critical to pair Maintain Clear Focus with Respect to make sure that you attend to both questions, "What's in it for me?" and "What's in it for them?"

When you are Relaxed, you need to be alert and ready, not limp and flaccid. In the film *Bad Day at Black Rock,* Spencer Tracy's character comes to town to fulfill a promise. The people of Black Rock have a secret, and they do all they can to taunt and threaten Tracy to get him to leave town. He responds calmly, using humor or ignoring the comments. He is never weak; he seems in control and relaxed. Finally, when he does need to defend himself, he is ready and he acts swiftly and effectively.

Although Joining with the Resistance is a critical part of the fifth touchstone, there are times when it is possible to join the wrong people. For example, when others are acting illegally, you could take this touchstone too far by joining in.

Sometimes it is best just to let resistance be. Woody Allen spoke of ruining his stand-up comedy routine by focusing entirely on people who heckled him. By doing so, he lost his timing and the laughter of those who thought he was funny. Please don't read this paragraph as the caveat that invalidates the book. That's not my intent. But there are times when you have a critical mass on your side, and there may still be some who continue to resist no matter what you do. In those cases, treat them with Respect, and move on.

If you use any of the touchstones in isolation from the others, you run the risk of using a potentially helpful guideline in a harmful way. If you consider strategies that incorporate most (or all) of the touchstones, you have a much greater chance of ensuring that your approach to the change will respect both your interests and others.

# 6 PUTTING IT ALL TOGETHER

Life is change. Growth is optional. Choose wisely.
—*Karen Kaiser Clark*

This is not a cookbook. The ideas mentioned so far, and those to follow, are not simply recipes. You would be better served to think of this book as the ingredients. How you put them together depends on the skills of the chef as well as on the menu of unique circumstances.

This chapter shows how you can use the cycle and touchstones to develop and reflect on strategies. The first example shows how one organization's major change adhered to the spirit of the cycle and the criteria of the touchstones. The second shows how an individual might apply those ingredients in combination.

## MAJOR CULTURAL CHANGE

The accounting firm of Deloitte & Touche LLP was concerned that it was losing many of its talented women. Talented people are crucial to a client service business. Something had to be done.

How Deloitte & Touche responded to this challenge provides a clear illustration of the common stages of change and ways to handle movement toward a goal using the touchstones.

The firm's initial assessment was that women were leaving to raise families; however, on deeper examination they found that only 13 percent had quit their careers. Some 65 percent of the women had left to take full-time jobs with clients, competitors, and other organizations; another 22 percent were working part time.

Once senior management recognized the problem, they assigned a group of partners to study the issue and make recommendations. Knowing their own culture well, they felt that using a mix of partners from throughout the firm to make the recommendations would broaden the base of support for whatever strategy they eventually adopted.

The partners recommended establishing an ongoing process that would encourage the retention and advancement of women. Since the firm makes its money by solving problems and completing projects, management and staff tend to view every issue as a project with a clear beginning and end and, once that project is completed, move on to the next assignment. Making the Women's Initiative an ongoing process would send a message that this project was different and would demand attention over a period of years. The partners believed the process would need strong leadership from the top of the firm, personal accountability among management staff, and highly visible communication regarding goals, strategies, and accomplishments.

The Women's Initiative evolved from a task force led by the firm's chairman and CEO, Mike Cook. Ellen Gabriel, a partner who was a member of the task force, was assigned to head the initiative. Former Secretary of Labor Lynn Martin was named to head an outside advisory board with carte blanche to examine practices and help keep the process on track.

In just over one year, virtually all partners and managers (about 5,000 people) had received a two-day orientation to this initiative. These sessions differed significantly from much that passes as diversity training. Although people did receive some instruction on communication skills and theory of gender issues in the workplace, most of the time was spent in conversations between men and women. The format provided a relatively safe way for people to talk about issues. And talk they did. Issues that had been taboo were now out in the open. The safe structure of the dialogue allowed participants to go beneath the surface and find out why people felt they way they did.

Not everyone left these sessions believing in the initiative, but many did. Some gained reassurance that others were concerned about issues important to them. For others, the sessions had the impact of a sledgehammer to the head—they saw things differently. They began to recognize the difficulties women faced in the workplace and what they could do to begin shifting to a more hospitable culture. After everyone received training, each practice office was expected to find its own way to encourage the advancement of women.

As I write this book, the Women's Initiative is on track at Deloitte & Touche. Although it is far too soon to pass final judgment on its effectiveness, there are signs of significant progress. The firm has implemented flexible work arrangements and reduced hours for all its people, including managers and partners. (These are key issues in retaining not only talented women but men as well.) In November 1994, the firm was recognized as a leader in promoting the issues of women in the workplace.[1]

## THE CYCLE

The Women's Initiative is moving nicely through the stages of the cycle. Women had been leaving the firm at a higher rate for years, but it was only recently that this was Recognized as an issue that needed attention. During the Random Incidents stage, individuals certainly saw the problem (none more so than the women who were actually leaving), but the full organization had not paid attention to this phenomenon.

Moving from Random Incidents to Recognition is like adding dots to a connect-the-dots picture. With two or three dots on the page, it is difficult to make much sense out of the picture. A few more dots and you may begin to guess at what you see. But once the page is filled with dots, you can begin to see the pattern—a picture develops.

In Deloitte & Touche's case, the number of talented women leaving, a heightened awareness about the changing nature of the work force, and concerns expressed by women who chose to stay with the firm were the dots that moved the cycle from Random Incidents to Recognition for most people.

The firm took Initial Actions by studying the issue further and not leaping to a quick-fix solution. This gave them more data, confirming that it was a real issue, and brought some others to Recognition. (Since accounting firms love numbers, data were an important factor in building awareness of the issue.)

The firm took its time finding a consultant who could develop a solid training program that would raise awareness throughout the firm.[2] The training firm they chose proposed a program to heighten recognition through dialogue—men to women, women to men. Even though the training included the obligatory action-planning stage, its real value was in how it provided a safe environment in which people could hear each other's stories.

Deloitte & Touche spent over a year working in Initial Actions, slowly building support for the change throughout the firm. (It's easy to be impatient with this stage. You want to move on quickly to Implementation and Integration. These early stages of the cycle are critical. Taking the time to build support reduces major resistance during Implementation.) Today, the company is working on Implementation. Offices around the country have developed plans that fit their unique situations. Since no two offices are the same, strategies will differ. Each office must, in effect, create its own cycle. It must Recognize the situation within its region. How many women are leaving? How many are being advanced? It must develop Initial Actions that fit its environment. And it must Implement those actions.

## USING THE CYCLE TO ANTICIPATE THE FUTURE

The firm is far from Integrating these ideas into the way it does business. It has set realistic goals of five to seven years to reach Integration. The goal will be met when women and men are being advanced in equal proportions without any special initiatives to guide them.

Using the cycle, you can anticipate some things that might occur and may therefore be worthy of their attention as they proceed.

### Change in Leadership

The process is moving from corporate headquarters to regional offices. This causes a break in the cycle as the focus shifts from national to local. During the first year and a half, there was considerable attention placed on the initiative, and pressure by the national office to attend the Men and Women as Colleagues course. The company must ask, Where will that same driving vision (Maintain Clear Focus) come from, now that the national office has less control over implementation?

### Continued Resistance

Those who are still resisting (and there are some) may feel they have weathered the storm. They survived the training by lying low or speaking the words of equality; now they can get back to work as usual. The firm needs to make certain it has a critical mass as it moves forward. Will the regions pick up the baton as it is passed to them? If the answer is yes (and it probably is yes), then the firm simply needs to support regional leadership. If the answer is no, it needs to develop ways to help regional offices make the move from Initial Actions to Implementation. For example, management might dig deeper, try to determine why people are still resisting, and find out what they need. "What's in it for them?" Perhaps seeing how other regions are

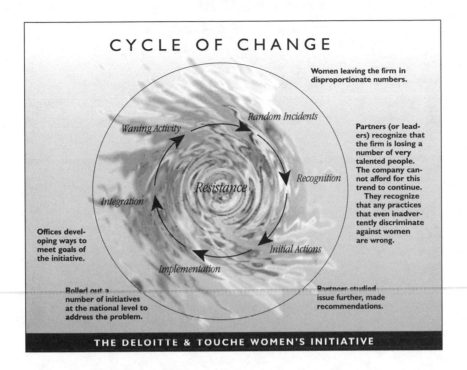

# CYCLE OF CHANGE

Women leaving the firm in disproportionate numbers.

*Random Incidents*

*Waning Activity*

Partners (or leaders) recognize that the firm is losing a number of very talented people. The company cannot afford for this trend to continue.
They recognize that any practices that even inadvertently discriminate against women are wrong.

*Recognition*

*Resistance*

*Integration*

Offices developing ways to meet goals of the initiative.

*Initial Actions*

*Implementation*

Rolled out a number of initiatives at the national level to address the problem.

Partners studied issue further, made recommendations.

**THE DELOITTE & TOUCHE WOMEN'S INITIATIVE**

implementing the initiative will reduce their fears. Even though the firm's leadership has said it many times before, some people may still need assurances that paying attention to women's retention and advancement will not result in quotas.

### *A New Cycle*
People are beginning to talk about hiring and retaining people of color. The firm must be careful not to assume that staff's Recognition of the importance of retention and advancement of women will automatically translate to an understanding of the issues in this broader arena. The firm will most likely need to approach this new challenge with equal rigor and commitment. Although the firm will certainly be able to learn a considerable amount from the Women's Initiative, any change in emphasis should be considered a new cycle. People will need to be brought on board and involved in the planning and implementation of this new cycle.

### *Two Steps Forward, One Step Back*
As much as the company might want progress to be linear, it may not happen. They need to be prepared for changing conditions. What will be clients' reactions to having women in senior positions? The effect may be positive, making it easier to move at full speed. But if clients react negatively, the firm needs to be prepared to respond to this challenge.

# HOW AN INDIVIDUAL
# CAN USE THE TOUCHSTONES

In an effort to be more responsive to the public, a government agency decided to adopt a quality improvement process. They held a conference to introduce these concepts to all the middle managers. They brought in an expert on one aspect of total quality management and asked him to speak to the group for two hours. He stood in front with a pile of overhead transparencies that was at least eighteen inches high. He said—and I am not making this up—"Normally this is a three-day presentation, so I'm going to have to go fast." Those of us in the back of the room could not read the fine print and graphs on the chart, and soon many were tuning out. He did nothing to engage the audience. Where were they on the cycle? Were they with him? Did they hate what he had to say? The speaker had no way of knowing. On a break, one woman turned to another and uttered Jane Wagner's wonderful line: "No matter how cynical I get, it's never enough to keep up."[3] She spoke for many in the room.

The expert's presentation failed to Embrace Resistance or show Respect for those in the audience. Had he used the touchstones as a guide, he might have developed a very different presentation. Imagine that he had held the following conversation with himself before the event:

"Maintain Clear Focus. My goal is to introduce total quality management to this group. I want to make sure they understand it. I must remember that my goal is not to convert the masses to my religion. I simply want them to understand what they might be getting into. Stay focused. Since I believe in this stuff, and I love the nuts and bolts of the work, I run the risk of losing my audience in the details. Make a few major points showing the benefits, the costs, the time, and the potential risks.

"Respect Those Who Resist. I don't know this group. Some may already have experience in this area. Some may be forced to attend. Some may be eager. Some may be cynical. I need more information about them. I need to

## Seeds of Destruction

Each stage of the cycle has in it the seeds of its own destruction. Implementation will not last forever. It will lead inevitably to either Integration or failure. Waning Activity could lead to renewal. For example, expanding the activity to include others in the organization would be a way of continuing the movement around the cycle. The firm will need to pay attention to the signs that it's time to move to the next stage.

find out where people are on the cycle. I will either gather some data beforehand or find a way to involve them right at the beginning to see where I stand. I must remember that their experience is their experience. From their points of view, resistance may be perfectly legitimate. I must make room for them to speak the truth as they see it. Knowing myself, I need to be careful not to rebut every statement.

"Embrace Resistance. I need to be interested in their resistance to this process. I have done these presentations before. I pretty much know the general areas of resistance, but I do need to learn why they might resist it here in this organization. Stay open to learning from them. Ask open-ended questions. Explore their answers.

"Relax. This will be the most difficult for me. I believe in quality improvement and I may go on the offensive. This will not help me meet my goal. What can I do? Prepare thoroughly, and that includes gathering as much information as I can about the client. Get there early and meet a few of the people. I am more at ease when I can look people directly in the eye or use their name. Cut back to a few key overheads to give plenty of time for questions, answers, and stories. Remember, if my job is to educate, all I need to do is leave them with information about the process. Senior management is only exploring the possibility of quality improvement, and besides, it will be their job—not mine—to try to implement it.

That quick internal monologue could have created a very different atmosphere. I have seen many speakers acknowledge the resistance in the room and give it credence—then, without denigrating or manipulating people, present to a more receptive audience. Of course people will still be skeptical—they should.

We don't want people to swallow everything whole. But their willingness to listen can change the atmosphere from cynicism to openness. And that is major progress.

Staying too long at one stage could decrease momentum and actually increase resistance—a common problem in many organizational change efforts. So far, Deloitte & Touche has avoided this pitfall. During the orientation stage the firm moved as swiftly as it could to provide training for every manager and partner. If they had stretched it out over two to three years, they would have lost momentum. By the time their offices got around to discussing the issue, the first people through the program would have forgotten about the insights and promises.

## USING THE TOUCHSTONES

Just as touchstones can be used to help individuals form strategy and stay on track, they are equally important in guiding action for the organization as well. The strategies employed in, say, Embracing Resistance may look different when used by an individual versus a full organization, but the impact is the same. Deloitte & Touche's Women's Initiative adheres to the five touchstones quite nicely.

### *Maintain Clear Focus*

The firm set direction from the top. Senior management understood and agreed to support the goal. They demonstrated this support by being the first to attend the training and by speaking publicly to groups of partners and managers.

They also took the long view. They knew that changing the culture would be difficult, so they set realistic long-range goals. The overall goal was clear; it was defined repeatedly by the firm's senior partners. I attended one meeting in which a partner flew from London to Phoenix just to speak briefly to a group of three hundred new managers on the importance of the initiative.

During that first year, the firm received a tremendous amount of attention in the business press. I believe this served two purposes: it was an affirmation by the business community that they were doing something worthwhile, and it kept attention on the process. No one could forget about this initiative, since it was never on the back burner. This also kept them focused, because a slip-up would get external exposure.

### *Embrace Resistance*

The two-day orientation training gave partners and managers an opportunity to explore the issues. These sessions were very important in allowing people a forum to discuss resistance (as well as their hopes) candidly.

### *Respect Those Who Resist*

Senior management set the goals but did not determine strategy for the offices. Whether out of necessity or design, this tactic put the power into the hands of the people who were to implement solutions.

The training was designed to allow people to speak honestly without being judged. Although this was difficult to achieve, the sessions were a safe forum in which the points of view of both women and men were treated with Respect. Most important, these sessions combined speaking with listening. Too often, corporate change agents forget that people must have a voice.

## Relax

The structure for the two-day sessions provided a degree of safety. Sessions were held off site; people dressed in casual attire. Within minutes after entering the training room, people could see that there was not going to be a reenactment of a 1960s-style, let-it-all-hang-out sensitivity session—no histrionics, no shouting, no group hugs. These were accountants and management consultants—rational people who like to work with their brains. The process needed to respect their world.

These orientation sessions could be seen as rituals. Rituals allow us to Relax because we know what's coming. We are assured that nothing strange will occur within the boundaries of that rite.

Another aspect of Relaxation was that senior management was prepared. They did their homework before launching this initiative. Preparation can allow an organization to Relax. It can help people feel less that the change is chaotic.

## Join with the Resistance

Although senior management never altered its goals, Implementation strategies have been developed by partners and managers within each region, allowing each office to adapt the process to fit its unique culture.

None of this is to suggest that Deloitte & Touche is unique or that the best uses of the cycle and the touchstones are limited to single-issue change initiatives. I include their story because it exemplifies getting people involved in a major change—even when they are already working long hours and meeting rigorous client demands. It would have been tempting for senior partners just to announce an executive decree. For whatever reasons, they chose a wiser and ultimately more beneficial alternative.

# PART II

*Assess the*
*Situation*

# 7 WHERE ARE YOU TODAY?

The key to everything is patience. You get the chicken by hatching the egg, not by smashing it.
—*Arnold Glasow*

Resistance often appears when people are at different points on the cycle. Take the time to compare the relative positions on the cycle held by everyone involved; it can help you anticipate potential problems and develop the most appropriate strategies.

## MOVING AGAINST THE TIDE

Imagine this scenario: The information systems (IS) department of a retail operation saw many ways new technology could serve the business by streamlining ordering and inventory procedures. They believed this would eventually reduce costs significantly. However, to realize these benefits, the company would need to invest heavily in technology during the first few years. IS saw what had to be done and how to do it. (Their vision was at the nine o'clock position, Integration.) Unfortunately for IS, other leaders in the company did not see the same picture. Although most senior management saw an important role for IS, they did not Recognize a need for such massive expenditures. (Senior management was at two o'clock, somewhere between Random Incidents and Recognition.)

IS leadership kept pushing. They became crusaders. In spite of their preaching, senior management did not suddenly "get it" and jump to nine o'clock. Instead, they became entrenched where they were on the cycle. They resisted what they perceived to be IS's arrogance. Their arrow dove into resistance.

If IS had stepped back and examined their different positions on the cycle of change, they might have taken a different course. They might have realized that they were far ahead of the people they wanted to influence. Senior management saw what it saw; no amount of browbeating or tugging would make them come along. IS might have been more successful had they sought ways to help senior management see the same picture of the role of technology, or tried to learn more about the pressures facing the leaders.

## MOVING WITH THE TIDE

Another information systems department, this one in a financial services institution, embarked on a major effort to fully automate all financial transactions using a single integrated system. The company had been using many different systems, making it difficult for people in New York to get timely information from their Tokyo office. Weeks would go by before critical financial data were translated so that each office could analyze performance. This was costly. If they could not monitor currency fluctuations in real time, they could lose millions in transactions.

IS leadership held a meeting of all key stakeholders to discuss their proposed plans and get input from others in the business. Even though IS had a vision (nine o'clock), they worked at one and three o'clock to make sure everyone saw the same picture. They convened first with the firm's senior management to explore the question "What's in it for them?" Later, at a retreat, they worked to get support and ideas from those who would eventually implement the changes.

The contrast in the way these two companies managed change speaks to the importance of having a way to anticipate resistance in order to develop strategies that build support for change.

## YOUR PLACE ON THE CYCLE

It is best to have a particular change in mind as you read this section. Either think about a change you tried to implement that didn't go as you had hoped, or consider a current change for which you are trying to build support.

The richness of the cycle comes in the potential tension between your position on the cycle and others'. I will write as if there were only one other group, so you will be looking at only two points on the cycle—where you are and where they are. Actually, there are probably many different groups, each with its own interests and position on your cycle. To thoroughly understand the situation, you would need to complete this quick assessment with each of the other key individuals or groups.

The three most common patterns are these:

- Way Out Ahead
- In It Together
- Stalled

Each has its special challenges and implications. By fully understanding these, you increase the probability that you will build support for the change.

### Way Out Ahead

This is the most common situation. You are far ahead of others. Although your vision may not yet be fully formed, it already puts you far from those who don't even recognize a need for change. Your challenge will be to hold onto your vision while working with others wherever they happen to be on the cycle (Touchstone No. 1: Maintain Clear Focus).

As you work, keep in mind the sheer distance between your relative views. These people are unaware of the need for change because they don't see the same picture as

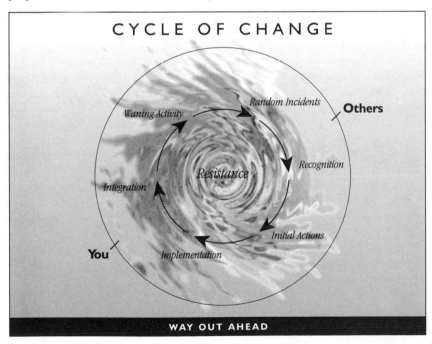

# CYCLE OF CHANGE

Random Incidents

**Others**

Waning Activity

Recognition

*Resistance*

Integration

Initial Actions

**You**

Implementation

**WAY OUT AHEAD**

you—not because they're out to get you. You are not necessarily brighter than they are; you simply see things differently. Since you have already gone through all the earlier stages and moved far around the circle in your own mind, you run the risk of staying out ahead and trying to force your idea on them. No matter how badly you want to get this idea implemented, you must back up and work with these people.

Ask yourself, Why do we see things differently? Is there anything I can do to help them see the need for change from my point of view? If I simply presented my picture of the possible vision, would this be enough?

Be prepared to learn from them. As you talk with them, you may learn things that change your view of the situation. In other words, your vision may change. You may also learn why they resist your idea. Keep open to exploration.

### IMPLICATIONS

If you stay out ahead and avoid working with others who are somewhere else on the cycle, you run the risk of adding bricks to the wall and strengthening resistance to your idea. The most common reason that change falters is an inability to hold a vision in mind while working with those at a different position on the cycle.

But there certainly are exceptions. Recall the story about Cinmade from chapter 5. What set Cinmade's case apart from most organizational changes was that profit sharing and employee involvement were good for the people, even if they didn't agree at the time. Robert Frey was able to persevere because he stuck to some

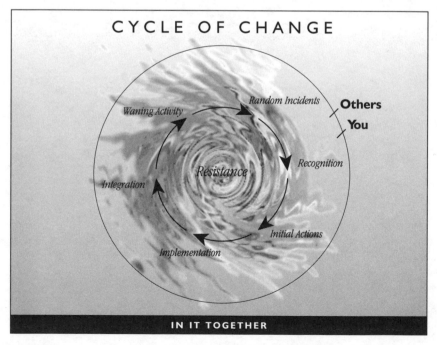

CYCLE OF CHANGE

Random Incidents

Waning Activity

**Others**

**You**

Recognition

Resistance

Integration

Initial Actions

Implementation

IN IT TOGETHER

of the touchstones. He Maintained Clear Focus, showed Respect for those who worked for him, and seemed to handle the almost constant resistance gracefully.

### IF YOU MUST STAY OUT AHEAD

Cinmade notwithstanding, staying out ahead is a risky stance. In effect, it suggests that you know best. Even if you are right, it can create tremendous resentment. Before proceeding, ask yourself:

- Why do I feel so strongly about my vision that I can't allow others to influence me?

- Is my vision in the best interests of the people who must support it? Am I sure?

- Even though my vision is set, is there any way I can get others involved in developing strategies?

If you choose to proceed without fully involving others, know that you will probably slog through a tremendous amount of resistance on the way to your goal. You have made a choice to abandon people who could be your allies, and the odds for success are not in your favor.

### In It Together

This is a great place to be. The other group and you are beginning to see something. Together you can explore what you see. Gather data. Hold focus-group meetings. Look at the competition. Examine quality reports and customer-service ratings. This is an opportunity for you and the other group to learn together. If you handle it well, you can move in tandem around the cycle.

Bringing together in a single setting all who have an interest in the proposed change has the advantage of ensuring that everyone hears the same thing and that the individuals and groups work together to create a common vision.

Here are some questions to ask:
- How can I get the others involved?
- How can I anticipate the resistance that may occur as we move around the cycle?

### IMPLICATIONS

By starting everyone at the same place on the cycle, you have an opportunity to build support for the change right from the beginning.

### Stalled

You can interpret placement at Stalled in two very different ways.

# A BALANCE OF FORCES

## AN INTERVIEW WITH JOHN CARTER

*John Carter is on the faculty of the Gestalt Institute of Cleveland and also an organizational consultant. I am impressed with his uncanny ability to articulate what's going on in organizations to clients. He has an E. F. Hutton quality about him: when he speaks, people listen.*

**RM:**  John, tell me what's your view of resistance?

**JC:**  Most people I work with see resistance as negative, but I see it as positive. I assume there needs to be some resistance as a balance of forces on anything that is taking place. Resistance is a good indicator of these forces. If I don't understand the balance of forces then I am unable to either influence the rate of change or the dynamics that are occurring in relation to that change.

I like to tell the story about Henry Ford. All of his advisors came in to get his approval on a project. His question to them was "What are the reasons for not making this change that you are suggesting?" They replied, "There aren't any." He told them to get out of his office, they hadn't done their home-work. They hadn't identified any reasons that might counter what they had come up with.

**RM:**  Do the forces always have to be balanced?

**JC:**  It is not a steady state, but there is always a balance. It's like flying an airplane. There's more resistance or less resistance—but always resistance.

**RM:**  It seems to me that hearing complaints is a good way to monitor those forces.

**JC:**  And yet a typical indicator of success is no complaints. I say the smaller the complaint, the better the job you have done. Most organizations want to wipe out the small complaint and tell people to only complain about big things. In mergers, I tell people to complain about whatever they have to complain about. Every time someone comes into your office and says, "I don't have a hook on the back of my door," thank them. Tell them it was wonderful that they brought that to your attention. "If there is anyone else out there with complaints like that, would you tell them to make sure to bring them to your attention?"

**RM:** Would you agree that working with resistance in the beginning of the change increases the likelihood that people will be committed to the change?

**JC:** Yes, by working with it on the front end you have fewer unintended consequences. There is a greater possibility that you will get the actual outcome you set out to get. You are able to focus more of your capacity on whatever your desired outcomes, rather than having them eaten up by managing and attending to unintended consequences.

**RM:** It would seem that paying attention to the balance of forces—getting resistance out on the table—would build commitment. How important is commitment?

**JC:** The only variable I can come up with that makes the primary difference is people's commitment to the change. There is no right or wrong way to bring about change. We can't absolutely know on the front end that a design is going to work. The basic difference between designs is how committed people are to them. You can take the absolute worst design, proved wrong in thirty other instances, but because people were committed to it, they made it work. And I've seen people take the best designs and mess them up royally.

1. **AGREEMENT ON STRATEGIES.** You are both at the same place on the cycle, and you see eye-to-eye on the best way to handle the proposed change. This agreement probably stems from a shared picture of the situation (Random Incidents and Recognition) and a common vision of what Integration would look like.

   The resistance that does occur will probably be over details (e.g., speed of implementation, budget, authority, responsibility) rather than any deeper issue. If you handle this situation well, the resistance will actually provide rich fodder for discussion as you progress through this cycle.

2. **CONFLICT OVER STRATEGIES.** You both recognize the problem facing you, and you may share common goals regarding successful outcomes, but you do not agree on a common approach. For example, you may prefer cost cutting, while the other group sees expanding the revenue base as a way to improve the bottom line. If you see a conflict over strategies, consider the following possibilities:

   - Resistance is likely to be over means rather than ends. Your preferred strategy may be wildly disruptive to the other group. Look for turf and power issues. What impact will the change have on the lives of those affected? Who wins and who loses?

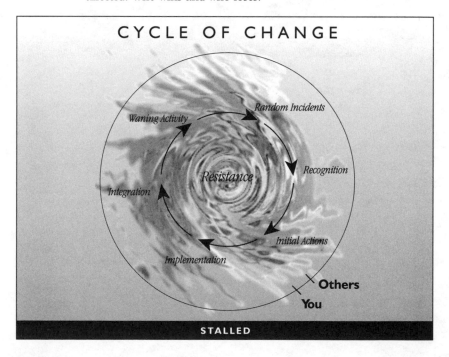

**CYCLE OF CHANGE**

Random Incidents

Waning Activity

Recognition

Resistance

Integration

Initial Actions

Implementation

Others

You

STALLED

- Keep reminding yourself and the others about the reason you are considering the change and what your goals are. This will help you keep things in perspective when you are immersed in minutiae such as trying to decide who gets a corner office.

## IMPLICATIONS

If the differences over strategies are deep and you fail to keep channels of communication open, resistance could intensify. However, since everyone agrees on the need for a change, this should not be a major problem.

## USING THE CYCLE

Identifying the other groups' placement on the cycle relative to yours is just the beginning. To use this framework for full effect, consider the following dynamics and nuances.

### *Each Stage of the Cycle Has Its Day*

If you move too fast, you will encounter resistance. The arrow should move clockwise around the cycle. When resistance occurs, the arrow leaves its orbit and falls toward the center of the circle. Deloitte & Touche is moving thoughtfully around the cycle, building support at each stage.

### WHO ARE THE PLAYERS?

It is important to identify all the people who have a stake in the change. Too often we limit this list to the usual suspects and forget key players and groups. When in doubt, think big.

If you're inside a large organization, consider the following individuals and groups. You may not need to include them all, but at least consider each before deciding who needs to be part of the planning.

- The chairman
- The board
- The chief executive officer
- The chief financial officer
- The chief operating officer
- Other execs and bosses
- External customers
- External suppliers
- Peers within your department
- Peers in other departments
- Your staff
- Internal customers (those who depend on you)
- Internal suppliers (those you must depend on)

Resistance will stop or hinder progress, divert your forward motion. Like a wrong turn on the highway, the diversion can take you miles off course. The more you disregard the dynamics of the cycle, the further people move into resistance.

Imagine this scenario. Management suddenly recognizes that the organization needs to reengineer the way it does business. Since a competitor introduced business-process reengineering with great success, management buys a one-size-fits-all process from Uncle Ed's Discount Consulting Warehouse and rolls it out a week later—going quickly from Recognition to Implementation.

Of course, staff are not at the same place on the cycle. They haven't heard about any problems that need to be engineered, much less reengineered. Before staff even Recognize that there is a problem, they are told to Implement this new process.

Since staff haven't seen the business reports, and tend to distrust management's interpretation of events, people are skeptical of this new idea. They believe that if they drag their feet or simply ignore management, this fad will pass like all the others before it. The harder management pushes to Implement quickly, the further everyone digs in.

### Always Ask, Am I Moving Too Fast?

If you take action now, will some group be left behind? If so, slow down. Implementation can come only when those whose support you need buy into the idea. Implementation should not occur until the self-interests of most parties are addressed so people can come together to create a new way of working.

Many new programs stall because key people who have a stake in the outcome are left out of the loop. All (or at least most) of the stakeholders must be brought into the planning and implementation process or you run a strong risk of never achieving full Integration. By spending a year building support, Deloitte & Touche have increased the chances that their people will not only Implement but Integrate the initiative into their day-to-day business practices.

### Anything Can Interrupt the Cycle

Stuff happens. Imagine that your merger is just beginning to take root when contract negotiations with the union begin at the newly acquired plant. Tension builds between management and staff. No matter how effective the process has been to date, the tension is likely to slow or stop progress. If you push ahead, you will almost certainly force a turn into resistance. Remember, anything can disrupt the cycle—news in the business press about a crisis in your industry, rumors of downsizing, someone on your team saying something so stupid that it ignites passions in the other groups.

Back up and explore ways to build common ground. You might ask everyone involved, Are there ways we can continue in spite of the tension building within the organization? If the answer is positive, work with all stakeholders to create workable strategies.

If tensions are so high that progress can't be made, back off, and wait out the storm. Once the air clears, back up to Recognition and explore the process again. Do not attempt to pick up where you left off. It may seem that things are the way they were before the storm, but the air is different, conditions have changed. To ignore this change invites resistance.

### Celebrate Resistance

When people resist, be thankful. Even if you hate what they have to say, these people have important things to tell you. Do whatever it takes to truly hear the reasons why people don't want to move ahead. Be curious and listen without judgment. Ask questions that help you plumb the depths. Don't punish those who tell the truth. Be thankful that someone had the courage to tell the emperor that he was dressed improperly for the parade.

Usually I am delighted to see resistance surface in meetings with clients. It's a sign of life. Once resistance is out in the open we can have a dialogue. But as long as people hold back, talk will be superficial and meaningless.

### Avoid Hoopla

Sometimes it is tempting to believe that banners, speeches, buttons, and geegaws trumpeting the new program will seduce people into signing on. The din of the band may be so loud that management may miss the fact that nobody else has joined the parade. These hollow celebrations may create a false belief that you are further along the cycle than you really are.

### Don't Hold Onto a Dying Program

Say a prayer, hold a funeral, then move on.

Allow the cycle to run its course. Never expect to arrive. Implementation and Integration are merely stops on the cycle. Just when everything seems to be working fine, someone will ask, "So what's next?" It would be easy to despair. However, the "What's next?" question indicates that the cycle is working and that it's time to take the change to another level.

Identifying everyone's position on the cycle is one step in your assessment. Now, turn to the second stage of the preparation: exploring the depth of the resistance.

# 8 HOW INTENSE IS THE RESISTANCE?

The most radical revolutionary will become a conservative
the day after the revolution.
—*Hannah Arendt*

T here is resistance and there is *resistance.* Knowing the intensity
can help you assess what you are getting into—and determine
whether you want to get into it at all.

Although some situations are so deeply embedded in organizations that cooperation seems impossible, most are not that bad. Unfortunately, the thought of resistance is so powerful that it may cloud your judgment, making it difficult to distinguish minor criticism from full-blown animosity. The more you know about the
intensity of the resistance facing you, the less likely that you will respond out of fear.

Think of resistance as degrees of intensity. Resistance moves from least to
most intense along a continuum. Although I arbitrarily divide this scale into

three levels for simplicity, it is important to think in terms of a rheostat that is infinitely adjustable.

## LEVEL 1: THE IDEA ITSELF

Level 1 is resistance to the change itself. There is no hidden agenda. People simply question or oppose the idea. Think of this as low-grade resistance. For example, say you want to paint the office fuchsia. People oppose the plan simply because they cannot abide that color. No hidden agendas, no deeper meaning lurking beneath the surface—they just hate fuchsia. Other Level 1 responses to the paint might be questions over cost or timeliness.

In Level 1, people oppose or don't move ahead for any of several reasons:

- They don't like the idea.
- They don't understand what you are trying to accomplish.
- They don't know why it is important to you.
- They believe in the status quo.
- They don't know what impact the change will have on them.
- They don't think you realize what this change will cost in money or time.
- They've got their own ideas about where the organization should go.
- They like your idea but think the timing is wrong.

Most articles and books on resistance deal with Level 1. They usually advise informing people about the change and getting them involved to some degree. Indeed, both are important for dealing with Level 1 resistance.

### Communicating the Idea

You may believe you can convince others by stating the situation from your own vantage point. A number of years ago I was in the market for a laptop computer. My only resistance to buying was minor: can I get what I need at a reasonable cost? Not knowing a lot about the workings of computers, I tuned out quickly when people launched into talk of bits and bytes. After several exasperating encounters with computer salespeople, I entered with some trepidation a store near my office. I assumed I would hear the same intimidating barrage of technical jargon, but this salesman was different. He asked what I wanted to use the laptop for. (No one had asked me that before.) I told him I needed to do word processing and send electronic mail. He seemed surprised. "That's it? That's all you need? Then this is what you want." He showed me a fairly inexpensive machine and assured me it would do what I wanted. No talk of esoteric computer stuff; he limited his remarks to addressing my question in English. I didn't shop around—I bought immediately.

That salesman did what so few of us do very well: listen and speak in other people's language.

### Getting Your Idea Across

In *The Diffusion of Innovations,* Everett Rogers identified five factors important in getting new ideas across to others.

1. **RELATIVE ADVANTAGE.** People need to see how change is better than the status quo. Information systems departments that set out to build strong computer systems often succeed by showing their companies why an investment today will pay off later.

2. **COMPATIBILITY.** People must see the link to the old way of doing things. For many years, the late Felix Grant was the preeminent jazz disc jockey in Washington, D.C. Radio station managers generally thought that jazz was too cerebral or ethnic for broad audiences. Grant realized that most station managers knew very little about music, so he called his show *The Album Sound:* "I dealt with them in the beginning by never using the word 'jazz.' I would play Sinatra, who was very big then, but I would play the hipper things that nobody else was playing…and the non-jazz fan for the most part wouldn't really know that it was jazz. He just heard good music, music that wasn't played much anywhere else. And it worked out very well. They sold a lot of spots and the station was happy."[1]

3. **SIMPLICITY.** As excited as you may be by the new idea, you must keep it simple. I believe that one of the reasons America Online, CompuServe, and Prodigy have been so successful is that they are easy to use. Other online services may offer similar features, but they are far more difficult to navigate.

4. **EASY TO TEST.** People need a chance to experiment with the new ways: What if I don't like it? What if it doesn't work? Rogers cites a 1943 study that found that all the Iowa farmers who adopted hybrid corn used it first on a trial basis. Widespread adoption would have been much slower without this trial period.

5. **OBSERVABILITY.** It's easier to accept something new after you've seen it in action. Many organizations, before adopting new technology in management systems, send staff on field trips to see how others are using it. During these trips, people can "kick tires" and ask tough questions. Rogers describes how people learn to accept innovations. Substitute "major change" for "innovation" and his comments are equally relevant. Although people do pay attention to objective studies or scientific evaluations, most people adopt an innovation only after seeing how it works for other people like them.

On the other hand, although people are most likely to accept innovations from people who are like them, most new ideas come from people who are different. It is their difference that lets them see things from another vantage point. It would be nice if they were alike in every way except the new idea, but they are usually quite different. "They simply do not talk the same language," writes Rogers.[2] This is why change agents must find common ground with those they hope to influence.

### Involvement

Getting people involved is the other principal advice that appears in so many articles on resistance. I agree completely with those authors: involvement is critical.

Although involvement seems simple enough, the most common corporate response to Level 1 resistance is to put on a show—tell them all about the change. The department head turns down the lights, pumps up the four-color-graphics slide show, and attempts to wow people into submission. Lights come up, the manager takes a few obligatory questions, then plans proceed at full speed. If all people needed were facts—Why this is important to you? What are your plans?—this approach might work. But if their Level 1 questions are a little deeper—How do I fit into this plan? Are you really serious about this change or is this another one of those fad-of-the-month-club ideas?—then these issues are not likely to be addressed by the wonders of presentation software.

This let's-put-on-a-show approach fails to incorporate at least two of the touchstones—Respect and Embracing Resistance. Presentations are one-sided: you talk, they listen. Even with long, thoughtful question-and-answer sessions, you are still the one with the answers.

This strategy fails to respect the potential contribution of those other people. Presentations seldom allow people to express their skepticism or concern in any meaningful way; most occur after all major decisions have been made. Dealing with people's resistance requires you to dive deep and explore until you are certain you have heard them. They just might have ideas that could make it a better project. Or they might be able to warn us of pitfalls.

### Risks of Level 1

Left unattended, Level 1 resistance can intensify. For example, if you push for Implementation while people are still questioning your sanity, they will dig in even harder.

A common fantasy is that once others see how good the change will be, they will move quickly around the cycle and join in. But you must ask yourself, When was the last time that happened? You must deal with the resistance as soon as we recognize it or else run the risk of allowing it to deepen.

# CYCLE OF CHANGE

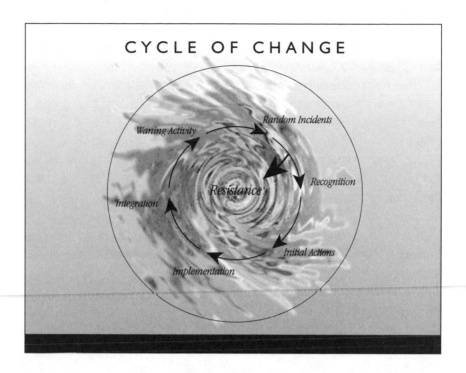

Most people fear dealing with resistance at any level. So even a simple Level 1 challenge like "We don't have enough staff to do that" may make you apoplectic. The slightest opposition may feel deep and intractable. You ascribe evil motives to the person who dared challenge you and respond with one of the common default approaches described in chapter 3, almost inevitably making matters worse.

## LEVEL 2: DEEPER ISSUES

Level 2 resistance is always deeper than the particular change at hand. It indicates that there are other forces at work. If you face opposition to painting the office fuchsia, you may learn that resistance has little to do with the color, and a lot to do with other—often unspoken—issues. This issues include distrust, bureaucratic culture, punishments and rewards, loss of respect and face, fear of loss, events in the world, and resilience. If conversations stay focused on the relative merits of fuchsia, you will miss learning about the true nature of the resistance.

Resistance is self-reinforcing. Just as it gets hotter near the center of the Earth, you pick up heat as you descend from the outer rim of the cycle. At Level 2, resistance becomes a force actively opposing your idea.

In organizations, most resistance is Level 2. This level of resistance manifests itself in several ways.

### Distrust

People believe they have been hurt in the past by you or the group you represent. In their minds, you have pushed through changes without regard for the human toll. They may believe you made promises that you later broke. In short, they don't trust what you say. They question your motives. They look for the hidden meanings. They read between the lines. They find malice in your every word, every action, every nuance.

Yet, there is hope. Even with some suspicion, you can work together and get things done. Often Level 2 relationships are built on contracts—explicit agreements that ensure that all sides will do what is promised.

Since trust is fairly low, anything can disrupt the change. People are likely to remain suspicious throughout the process, wondering if you are up to something. Rumors of a layoff, a wildcat strike, a contentious grievance settlement—almost anything can strengthen the resistance.

### Bureaucratic Culture

In traditional organizations, replete with many layers of reporting, people often feel powerless. And well they should; these bloated dinosaurs stifle creativity and ambition. Consider the middle manager in a federal agency who must ask permission to speak directly to managers two levels above him, even though his job is to organize professional meetings for these people.

People survive in bureaucracies by lying low and keeping things predictable. They measure success by the amount of power they can amass—for example, by controlling crucial information. Change upsets that balance; it often exposes people, and it most certainly disrupts life as usual. Peter Block writes that organizations create dependency, and with that, a sense of entitlement. The worker says, in effect, I will give up my autonomy if you will assure me a salary and a stable work environment.[3] This attitude does battle with any idea that threatens the status quo, or upsets the fragile implicit contract by exposing the person to failure. Although senior managers often speak disdainfully about bureaucrats, they must remember that organizations created the conditions that allow bureaucracy to flourish. For years (and in many places even today) organizations wanted yes men who would toady up to the boss. Now they want risk takers. It took years to create this mess; it will take many more before managers believe that senior management wants to change it.

Bureaucrats aren't born; they are cultivated. When you try to change a calcified system, remember that from their vantage point, resistance is justified. Your proposed change upsets the implicit contract.

### Punishments and Rewards

If what gets rewarded gets done, it is also true that what gets punished gets avoided.

People will resist change that runs counter to organizational rewards and punishments. One company I worked with wanted to revise an outmoded billing system in which a typical bill moved through many departments on its way to the customer. The process was slow and error prone. The vice president in charge of all the departments asked each group to assign a representative to a task force to do something about the problem.

During the first meeting, people talked about how important this issue was. They said, "It's about time we did something." But at the second meeting, people came late and left early. By the third meeting, people were sending substitutes. At the fourth meeting, I asked, "So, what's going on? You said this was important, and yet we begin late, end early, and never have the same players in the room."

The department representatives replied that, while this was an important action, they were given no credit for participating. Work was piling up on their desks; they would risk poor performance reviews if they gave too much time to this project. The internal rewards and punishments worked against the conditions needed for change.

### Loss of Respect and Face

People need to maintain their dignity. Often a change threatens this strong human need. The change may result in a loss of status, power, or control—a loss of face. When one construction company tried to implement quality improvement, a superintendent asked, "Do you mean to tell me everything we've been doing up till now ain't been worth nothing, and *now* we're going to have quality?"[4]

From the superintendent's point of view, this change was going to be a repudiation of his life's work. He was not resisting quality per se; he was resisting the strong personal blow to his self-esteem.

### Fear of Isolation

Fear of isolation also may occur when people feel excluded. The need to feel part of something is strong in us all. When we believe that we will be cast out as a result of change, we resist. The need to be included is so deep that we may not be aware of it leading our actions. Although the resistance may come out in a variety of ways—in-your-face criticism, silence, malicious compliance—it may never tell you that the concern is really one of needing to belong. Unless you can find ways to hear this fundamental human concern, you run the risk of solving the wrong problem.

The extreme form of this fear, quite common today, is fear of losing one's job. This is not just an economic loss (although that would be bad enough), but a threat to who we say we are. This loss robs us of our identity. When resistance is born of this kind of fear, people need support, not slick presentations.

### Events in the World

The world does not begin and end at the door of your place of business. A hospital administrator notices that articles in the press about the crisis in health care—downsizing, out-sourcing, mergers—have an impact on changes that she tries to implement. People are leery that these changes are really the start of something bigger and deeper. These outside events have an impact on the administrator's ability to get things done.

### Resilience

The pace of change in many organizations is so fast and chaotic that people may be worn out. They don't necessarily resist a particular change, they just can't imagine taking on something new.[5] When resilience is low, resistance comes from the cast of chronic fatigue—people are just plain beat.

### What's Needed

Level 1 concerns are primarily intellectual. Once people understand the change or get a voice, they go along with the new idea. Level 2 resistance, on the other hand, springs from the heart and the gut. Fear of isolation is not rational, nor does loss of face lend itself to a quick pep talk. If I think I'm going to lose my self-esteem (not to mention my home), I need to be:

- **ACTIVELY INVOLVED.** Level 2 concerns will not be resolved during a single focus-group meeting. People silently scream, "I need to feel part of my destiny. I want a hand in shaping the change that will affect me." What is called for is deep involvement in the process. Those who resist need to feel they can influence what happens in their own lives.

- **HEARD.** When resistance is deep, people wish to say to you: I need you to truly hear my concerns. I want you to hear what I don't have the words to say. I want you to stick with me until I can find those words.

- **VALUED.** In Level 2, people feel vulnerable. They feel as if their world may soon come crashing down. They need to know that those in charge care about them and will protect them.

### The Risk of Level 2

You may try to deal with deeper levels of resistance by using Level 1 strategies, but such superficial approaches cannot get at people's concerns and yearnings. Personal fear and yearning are not in the vocabulary of most business organizations. As you get close to these emotionally charged feelings, your tendency is to run, or to blame those who resist—not because they are resisting but because you cannot imagine engaging them at so deep a level. Meeting people at Level 2 takes courage.

During one meeting I attended, a CEO said that he had just ordered his head of human resources to lay off a number of staff—and that "as soon as he gets that done, I'm going to fire his ass too." I believe his crass insensitivity masked an inability to make human contact with his staff. He had to send an emissary to do his dirty work and then, to isolate himself from the pain, "fire his ass" as well. (Note that he couldn't even dignify the person with a name, only a body part.)

If you allow yourself to stay removed from the human toll, you cannot build support for your ideas. In the example above, those remaining will undoubtedly fear that the same thing could happen to them.

### LEVEL 3: DEEPLY EMBEDDED

This is the deepest, most entrenched form of resistance. The problems are big and may appear overwhelming. In the painting-the-office example, people view you as the enemy. In Level 3, they could love fuchsia and still oppose your idea simply because you—the enemy—came up with it. There are three major reasons why Level 3 occurs: a combination of Level 2 factors, historic animosity, and conflicting values and vision.

### Combination of Level 2 Factors

When Level 2 issues, such as fear of loss, occur repeatedly, resistance may increase to Level 3. People may now believe that they are without hope. They believe they have lost (or will lose) everything. Bottom looks like up.

Level 2 issues occurring in combination and over a long period of time may also deepen resistance. For example, if you (or the group you represent) have been guilty of repeated breaches of trust, confidence in you will be eroded. The worse the deception, the more likely people will view you through the lens of Level 3.

### Historic Animosity

Distrust is deeply entrenched. Often the hurt goes back years, perhaps even generations. Some management–labor relationships have not improved since the growth of the labor movement in the early part of this century. When a former chairman of the ill-fated Eastern Airlines was once asked what he thought of employee involvement, he replied, "There is no way I'm going to have the monkeys running the zoo."[6] This kind of arrogance makes cooperation extraordinarily difficult, if not impossible.

### Conflicting Values and Visions

What you want and what they want are far apart. Your goals appear to be in direct opposition to theirs. If you say up, they are sure to say down.

When historic animosity meets conflicting values and vision, Level 3 is extremely difficult to deal with. And yet, even in Level 3, there is hope. Since the early 1980s, many organizations and unions have found ways to forge new relationships and build partnerships that serve the interests of both management and labor.

In 1993 Yitzhak Rabin and Yasir Arafat shook hands on the White House lawn, signaling a new era in Middle Eastern politics. But it was just the beginning. Progress will be halting, like walking in a mine field. Even before the tragic assassination of Prime Minister Rabin, there had been setbacks. Firmly embedded resistance on all sides will make this a long and perilous journey.

There are no guarantees with Level 3 resistance. But there is hope. The Common Ground Network for Life and Choice brings together pro-choice and pro-life advocates for dialogue.[7] I can think of few hotter or more polarized issues in this country, but the Network is often successful in helping people find common ground. It is not uncommon for people to enter these meetings believing that they have nothing in common. Through dialogue, participants at these workshops learn that, although they disagree on the issue of abortion, there are many other issues where they do share common concern. For example, people find that both sides are concerned about the welfare of children, the status of women, and the growing numbers of unwanted pregnancies and abortions.

Once people recognize the common ground, they can begin to find ways to work together. In Buffalo, both sides search for strategies to reduce the number of unintended pregnancies. In other cities pro-life and pro-choice advocates have joined forces to address child welfare issues and the drug epidemic.

The major issue of whether or not abortion is right and should be legal will not be solved by these meetings. But their ability to identify areas where they can work together, and in the process learn to humanize and respect the other people, is a major accomplishment. If people on both sides of this hot issue can find ways to cooperate, surely corporations could do the same.

### Actions

Level 3 strategies are similar to those of Level 2, but require tremendous determination and persistence. If the conflict between yourself and another group is this deeply embedded, then you must ask yourself, Is it worth the effort? Success will probably take a very long time. After forty years in the wilderness, Moses never got to see the Promised Land himself. You must determine whether, realizing that you might never see its end yourself, you are willing to start something that massive.

### *The Risk*
Anything can go wrong when you walk in the Level 3 minefield. Trust is so low and the animosity so deep that the slightest misstep can set progress back months or years. It is especially tempting to quit mid-journey and revert to default strategies. Better not to have attempted anything than to have to use force against the other parties.[8]

## INTERPLAY OF THE LEVELS
The levels play off each other. You can make matters worse: you can intensify resistance by ignoring or treating Level 1 concerns flippantly. For example, once someone gives her point of view, she has made a commitment to something. She has marked off turf and now must defend it. In other words, before speaking she may have had little resistance, but once she has gone on record in front of her colleagues, they now have face to defend. This drives resistance deeper.[9]

Once you move from Level 1 into the deeper levels of resistance, finding common ground gets much more difficult. The lesson is to take lightly words spoken to you, and take your own words seriously. If people call you "the enemy," see it as a tactic until you know otherwise. But, in turn, be careful not to add to the resistance by responding in kind. A tit-for-tat verbal response is guaranteed to drive their arrow, as well as your own, deeper into the resistance.

## BEGINNING THE CONVERSATION
Use the Support for Change questionnaire to begin a dialogue about the degree of support you enjoy for the change. It covers eight major issues:
- Values and vision
- History of change
- Cooperation and trust
- Culture
- Resilience
- Rewards
- Respect and face
- Status quo

The reliability of the scores depends on who takes part in the discussion. If you limit the survey to the senior management team, you will probably get a skewed view of reality. Better to get data from a cross section of the organization in order to get a more complete picture.[10]

Responses to the questionnaire will act as a springboard for conversation about change and resistance. The actual scores will be less interesting than the reasons people scored it the way they did. Conversations should focus on the stories that accompany these scores. For example, if the CEO rates everything a seven (high), middle-manager scores range from three to five, and non–management staff rate everything low, you have the makings of a very intriguing conversation.

The purpose of the conversation is to bring opinions and feelings into the open. Obviously, your skill at facilitating dialogue (finding meaning through words) is critical.

### A Format for Conversation

Here is a format for working with the Support for Change questionnaire.

1. **GIVE THE QUESTIONNAIRE TO A CROSS SECTION OF THE ORGANIZATION.** (This need not be a large group as long as the scores reflect the range of opinions to whatever change is being considered.) Make certain that you do not overlook individuals or groups who may be critical to the success of the change. (It is easy to dismiss or conveniently forget to include people who continually object to your ideas. Their voices are crucial.)

2. **GO OVER THE SCORES BEFORE SHOWING THEM TO OTHERS.** This will allow you to react in the privacy of your office before facing others.

3. **CONVENE A MEETING OF ALL INTERESTED PARTIES.** Post scores on large sheets of flip chart paper, slides, or overheads. Ensure anonymity for individuals, but break out the scores by stakeholder groups. For example, use one color to indicate scores made by senior management, another color for middle managers, and so forth.

4. **EXPLORE THE RESULTS.** Ask questions based on your review of the "Interpretation" section. However, no matter what the scores are, there are a few questions you should consider asking:
   - What interests you about the scores?
   - Where do you see patterns?
   - Where are the points of greatest agreement?

> **HIGH SCORES = HIGH SUPPORT FOR CHANGE**
>
> **LOW SCORES = LOW SUPPORT AND HIGH RESISTANCE**
>
> **MID-RANGE SCORES = PROBABLE RESISTANCE**

- Where are the points of greatest disagreement?

Encourage people to explain why they scored the way they did. It is important to allow people to remain silent. However, when people do speak, create a non-threatening atmosphere so that they can describe the reasons for their scores. This will be especially important if most scored at one end of the scale and only one or two people scored on the other end. Some may try to convert their colleagues; don't allow this to happen.

5. **ACT.** Once you have explored the reasons behind the scores, ask the following questions:

- What are the implications of these scores for this change?

- If you proceed with the change, what must you do to begin to build support for it?

- How can you get people actively involved in the change process?

- How can all individuals and groups be treated with dignity and respect during the planning and implementation of the change?

## INTERPRETATION

Here are a few things to consider when interpreting the results of the questionnaire.

### *Numbers Need Explanation*

Even though 1, 2, and 3 should be considered low scores, 4 and 5 mid-range, 6 and 7 high, these are just numbers. One person's 5 is another's 3. The value lies in understanding the meanings people give to their scores.

Generally low to mid-range scores should be cause for concern. Lower scores indicate fertile soil for the growth of resistance.

# THE HAND ON THE OTHER SIDE OF THE WALL
## AN INTERVIEW WITH
### ADRIENNE KAUFMANN AND MARY JACKSTEIT

*Adrienne Kaufmann and Mary Jacksteit are co-directors of the Common Ground Network for Life and Choice. They facilitate dialogue between pro-life and pro-choice groups. They do amazing work in an area where people may see each other as enemies and where there would seem to be no common ground.*

**RM:** Why would people call you?

**MJ:** Usually there is a crisis, something has shocked people. They see hatred and lack of communication all around them, and none of the actions they know about seem to offer an effective approach to the problem.

**AK:** Or it might be a dissatisfaction with what's going on—they haven't gotten anyplace in twenty years!

**RM:** How do things get started?

**AK:** We insist that representatives from both sides of the issue sponsor the event. Someone might call and say they don't know anyone on the other side—they really do live in separate worlds. We help them get in touch with their counterparts on the other side of the issue.

**RM:** What happens during one of these dialogues? Do you use a standard design for these meetings?

**MJ:** Our manual explains the basic model but it is not a cookie cutter.* We work with local people to get their input. But the basic element—small group conversations facilitated by people who have been oriented to what we are trying to do—is standard. In small groups we ask people to talk about their personal experience—story telling rather than stating positions. The first key question is: What are personal experiences in your life that have led you to the position you now have on abortion?

**AK:** You can't argue about a person's experience. The key is that people on the other side have to actively listen. That experience builds a foundation for further work. Often these stories involve pain and that is where people can connect. We all understand pain.

**MJ:** The next questions often are, How are you stereotyped as a pro-life or pro-choice person?

How do you not fit that stereotype? And how do you feel about that? They can hear that they are feeling the same rage over being stereotyped.

**AK:** We are trying to humanize the others so that they are not just abstract stereotyped enemies but real people.

**RM:** It sounds like these questions are essential.

**MJ:** There are millions of books written on problem solving, but if you are talking about stuff that is shaking people to the core, you've got to treat it differently. We don't ask questions just as some warm fuzzy exercise. It is building a foundation for doing hard work. It's being clear where your differences are and not glossing over things.

**AK:** One woman told us, "When I thought about coming to this day, I pictured a wall of oozy, gooey, yucky slime, and I felt I was going to be asked to put my hand through. I did and I found a hand on the other side reaching for mine."

**RM:** So what allows people to find that hand on the other side of the wall?

**AK:** People find common ground. They don't try to convert each other, but they find areas where they can work together. For example, they often share a concern for the welfare of women and children in our society and the number of unwanted pregnancies.

**MJ:** They often begin to find ways they can work together on these common ground issues.

**RM:** Are you hopeful about your work?

**AK:** When I review some of the relationships that have been built over the past two years, it's very heartening.

**MJ:** This process makes them feel better about themselves. People say, "I feel good about what I am doing. I feel better as a human being." It is empowering.

\*   See Resources section for information on this manual.

### *Look for Patterns*

Are scores clustered together on particular items? If so, this probably indicates that most people agree about support for change on that scale.

Are the scores split? Perhaps non–management staff consistently rate things low while supervisors rate things high.

A pattern of high scores may indicate that the resistance will be Level 1—resistance limited to the change itself. The culture and history are probably such that people feel free to speak their minds. Therefore, conversations about the change should be easier to facilitate.

A pattern of low scores indicates deep (probably Level 3) concerns. You must take these concerns seriously. Take a long-range view of change; get people involved, and begin building bridges.

Any low or mid-range scores indicate resistance waiting to happen.

Mid-range scores may indicate that there are concerns deeper than the change itself (Level 2). It will be important to get these issues out on the table for discussion.

There are no right or wrong answers. Scores merely reflect people's perceptions.

### *Item Analysis*

Examine each item on the questionnaire. Use the following explanations to form questions to ask during the meeting.

1. **VALUES AND VISION.** Low scores could indicate Level 3 concerns. Values may be in conflict; individuals and groups may not see any common ground. This is serious. It almost guarantees that any major change will be resisted unless people learn how to begin building a shared set of values. On the other hand, low scores may indicate a communication problem. In some organizations, values and visions remain secret. People don't know where the organization is going. This is a communication problem and may not indicate deeper potential resistance.

2. **HISTORY OF CHANGE.** Low scores indicate a strong likelihood that this change will be resisted with great force. Those who want the change will need to demonstrate repeatedly that they are serious this time. People are likely to be very skeptical, so persistence will be critically important.

3. **COOPERATION AND TRUST.** Low scores probably indicate Level 3 concerns. This should be taken seriously. It is difficult, if not impossible, to build support for any major change without some degree of trust. The

opposite of trust is fear, therefore a low score means not just the absence of trust but the presence of fear.

4. **CULTURE.** Mid-range to low scores indicate that it may be difficult for people to carry out the changes even if they support you. They are saying that the systems and procedures hinder change. The change agents must be willing to examine these deeper systemic issues.

5. **RESILIENCE.** Low to mid-range scores probably indicate that people are burned out. Even though they may see the need for this change, they may have little strength to give to it. Two important questions: Is this change really necessary at this time? If so, how can you support people so that the change causes minimal disruption?

6. **REWARDS.** Obviously, low scores indicate strong potential resistance. Who in their right mind would support something that they knew would harm them? If their perceptions are accurate, then the change agents have a difficult challenge: How can they move forward with the change and find ways to make it rewarding for others? If the low scores indicate a misperception, then the change agents must let people know why they are misinformed. It is likely that this message will have to be communicated repeatedly (especially if trust is low as well).

7. **RESPECT AND FACE.** Low scores probably indicate potential Level 2 concerns. The change agents must find ways to make this a situation in which all can win.

8. **STATUS QUO.** Low scores indicate that people view this change as very disruptive and stressful. The more people get involved in the change process, the less resistance they are likely to experience. Most often people resist change when they feel a loss of control.

## SUPPORT FOR CHANGE QUESTIONNAIRE

This questionnaire is designed to help people understand the level of support or opposition to change within the organization.

### 1. *Values and Vision*
**(DO PEOPLE THROUGHOUT THE ORGANIZATION SHARE VALUES OR VISION?)**

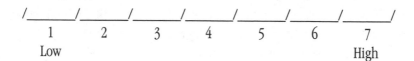

```
/_____/_____/_____/_____/_____/_____/_____/
   1      2      3      4      5      6      7
  Low                                      High
```

### 2. *History of Change*
**(DOES THE ORGANIZATION HAVE A GOOD TRACK RECORD HANDLING CHANGE?)**

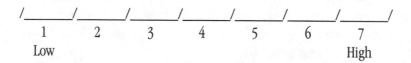

```
/_____/_____/_____/_____/_____/_____/_____/
   1      2      3      4      5      6      7
  Low                                      High
```

### 3. *Cooperation and Trust*
**(DO THEY SEEM HIGH THROUGHOUT THE ORGANIZATION?)**

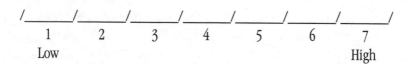

```
/_____/_____/_____/_____/_____/_____/_____/
   1      2      3      4      5      6      7
  Low                                      High
```

### 4. *Culture*
**(IS IT ONE THAT SUPPORTS RISK TAKING AND CHANGE?)**

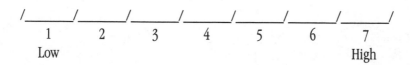

```
/_____/_____/_____/_____/_____/_____/_____/
   1      2      3      4      5      6      7
  Low                                      High
```

### 5. *Resilience*
**(CAN PEOPLE HANDLE MORE?)**

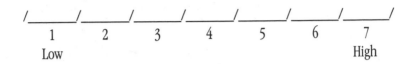

|   |   |   |   |   |   |   |
|---|---|---|---|---|---|---|
| 1 | 2 | 3 | 4 | 5 | 6 | 7 |
| Low |   |   |   |   |   | High |

### 6. *Rewards*
**(WILL THIS CHANGE BE SEEN AS BENEFICIAL?)**

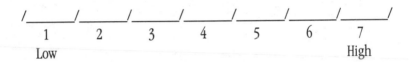

|   |   |   |   |   |   |   |
|---|---|---|---|---|---|---|
| 1 | 2 | 3 | 4 | 5 | 6 | 7 |
| Low |   |   |   |   |   | High |

### 7. *Respect and Face*
**(WILL PEOPLE BE ABLE TO MAINTAIN DIGNITY AND SELF-RESPECT?)**

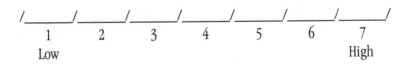

|   |   |   |   |   |   |   |
|---|---|---|---|---|---|---|
| 1 | 2 | 3 | 4 | 5 | 6 | 7 |
| Low |   |   |   |   |   | High |

### 8. *Status Quo*
**(WILL THIS CHANGE BE SEEN AS MILD?)**

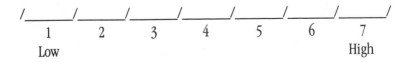

|   |   |   |   |   |   |   |
|---|---|---|---|---|---|---|
| 1 | 2 | 3 | 4 | 5 | 6 | 7 |
| Low |   |   |   |   |   | High |

# 9 WHAT'S YOUR CONTRIBUTION TO THE PROBLEM?

Everyone thinks of changing the world,
but no one thinks of changing himself.
—*Tolstoy*

We have met the enemy, and he is us.
—*Pogo (thanks to Walt Kelly)*

A s much as we might hate to admit it, Tolstoy and Pogo were right.
We are the enemy. Our default reaction—how we resist those
who resist us—sometimes creates and almost always increases
opposition to our ideas. Even if the change involves a cast of
thousands and is played out on a world stage, it begins with individuals. What we say, how we say it, our tone of voice, our style, all can make matters worse or begin to build support.

This self-assessment is the key to the book. We cannot deal with resistance in
others without first examining ourselves. As Gandhi said, "We must become the
change we wish to see in the world." So, why did I place this chapter so late in the
book? In a study I conducted, managers assessing their own skills in dealing with
resistance tended to overrate themselves. By placing the look inward this late in the

book, I hoped that readers would be more receptive to looking at themselves candidly. That is, I was just trying to build a little support for a change in thinking.

We seldom look inward when we talk of resistance. We can identify in a heartbeat how *they* are resisting *us,* but it is much harder for us to see that we are a critical partner in the dance as well. We see those other people as the wayward souls. We, after all, are simply trying to promote truth, justice, and the company way.

If we fail to see how our style may actually create needless resistance or how our reactions turn Level 1 issues into deeply entrenched Level 2 opposition, we are doomed to repeat the same halting dance again and again.

Before we can change our behavior, we must first recognize what we are doing currently to contribute to the problem.[1] In this chapter, I invite you to take that sobering look inward.

## PERSONAL RESISTANCE STYLE

Here is a self-assessment. I encourage you to slow down your reading and consider how you would respond to each of these questions. I firmly believe that we cannot hope to work effectively with resistance unless we recognize our contribution to the game. To prime the pump, and help you see how to approach this assessment, I have included a hypothetical example of a hospital CEO who is facing major changes in his organization.

Move slowly through the self-assessment, and carefully consider your responses to each question.

### 1. Consider a Past Change

Consider a big change that was killed or seriously hurt by resistance—a change in which you were a major player. Write the history of the change as dispassionately as possible. Don't make judgments. Don't use adjectives or expletives. Just write the facts.

The following questions ask you to consider your movement through the cycle of change. Since this is a change that failed, the questions stop just before Integration.

- **RANDOM INCIDENTS.** When did you first become aware of issues that needed to be addressed?

  *Hospital CEO: The 1992 presidential election brought health care to the table. After the election, press coverage increased tenfold. Many articles covered rising costs and inefficiencies in health-care management. At the same time, similar hospitals around the country began seeking to form alliances with physician groups and other ancillary services. There was some talk of mergers of larger hospitals.*

- **RECOGNITION.** When did you see that you had to do something? Who else Recognized the same problem or opportunity?

*Two of our major competitors were beginning to talk about collaborating. I knew that we had to act immediately or else risk losing market share to other large players.*

- **INITIAL ACTIONS.** What were the first steps you took? Who did you involve in those early actions?

*I called together the senior management team—the chief financial officer, the chief operating officer, and the vice presidents for nursing and medical services. We agreed that we needed to do something as soon as possible. Over the next few weeks we identified the players who were likely to be interested in joining us. We decided to open talks with two smaller hospitals (Hospitals A and B), a nursing home, and a newly formed physicians group.*

*We held meetings with the other facilities. Hospital B was not interested, but all the other groups were interested in pursuing this.*

*These initial steps took approximately four months.*

- **IMPLEMENTATION.** Did you attempt to enact the plan?

*In late 1993, we announced the formation of a consolidated healthcare system. By this time another hospital (Hospital C) had asked to join us. Our alliance accepted them into the group.*

At what point in the cycle did the project die?

*The project fell apart during Implementation. Hospital C quit the alliance shortly after implementation and joined a larger competitor.*

### 2. How Did They Resist?

List all the ways in which others resisted the change. Be specific, and list as many incidents as you can recall.

*Hospital C was critical of the Implementation plan from the moment they joined us. They seemed particularly concerned over our fast pace. We seemed to fight constantly with the executive team from Hospital A.*

*Our fights were usually over who would take primary responsibility for setting strategic direction and day-to-day operations. Since we were the larger facility, we argued that we should take primary leadership. They never agreed with us. . . . To the surprise of our executive team, our staff made Implementation difficult. They were reluctant to share resources or information with Hospital A. And due to a front-page newspaper article on downsizing in the industry, a rumor spread among our staff that the new alliance would mean fewer jobs. . . .*

*Hospital A had a strong reputation in maternity, and their staff, in turn, seemed unwilling to share "secrets" with our staff. . . .*

*Almost every day, I got wind of people's dissatisfaction. Change was occurring too fast, too slow, wasn't needed, or was being handled insensitively. It seemed no one was happy with the change or my leadership style!*

### 3. How Did You React to Them Internally?

Look for the triggers. Go back through the assessment and identify what happened immediately after each incidence of resistance.

**THOUGHTS.** What were your first thoughts? People often come to one of the following conclusions:

- You blame them for resisting you.
- You blame yourself for choosing such a stupid strategy.
- You swallow their criticism, and without thinking, accept their view.
- You fail to grasp the significance of or don't let yourself pay attention to what they are saying or doing.

*When resistance occurred within the other facilities, my first thought was to dismiss it as natural growing pains. Meetings are always difficult. Why should talk of a merger be any different? . . . When our staff dragged their feet, I silently blamed them for not caring about the health of our hospital. And I thought they were stupid or had their heads in the sand.*

**FEELINGS.** What were your feelings about what occurred? For example, you might have felt

- **ANGER.** You were outraged at their reaction.

- **BETRAYAL.** You were deeply hurt by their letting you down.

- **CONFUSION.** You didn't know what you felt. Thoughts and feelings rushed together in a blur.

- **RELIEF.** They told you what you needed to hear and saved you embarrassment and frustration.

> *I was angry at Hospital C for leading us down the garden path. They said they were in and then they betrayed us. . . .*
>
> *As things progressed, I found myself getting angry at everyone. I even started snapping at my executive team—and they were on my side!*
>
> *Finally, I was hurt. How could so many people, especially my staff, let me down?*

**PHYSICAL.** You probably reacted physically when others resisted you. You may have found yourself feeling

- **NAUSEOUS.** Your digestive tract erupted, giving you an acid bath.

- **SLEEPY.** You found it difficult to keep listening to the others. You got drowsy.

- **SLEEPLESS.** You couldn't stop thinking or reacting to their resistance.

- **MUSCLE TENSION.** You may have felt parts of your body, perhaps your neck and shoulders, tighten.

> *It started with mild headaches. Then I couldn't sleep. I don't sleep well as it is, but I would be awake for hours every night thinking about the merger. My diet went to hell and I quit exercising. All I could do was think about this problem.*

Your internal reactions can be powerful. If you are unaware of them, they can limit your ability to respond effectively to others. In Robert Louis Stevenson's *Doctor Jekyll and Mister Hyde,* the kind and generous doctor would allow himself to see only the part of himself that he thought was good. His tragedy was not that he harbored evil thoughts, but that the only outlet came in the form of the monstrous Mister Hyde.

The less aware you are of your internal reactions, the more likely Mister Hyde will take over. Understanding and accepting how you react when others oppose you gives you options. Knowing yourself allows you to choose among alternatives.

### 4. How Did You React Externally?

List how you reacted to each sign of resistance as it occurred. Since it is usually far easier to recognize the resistance in others than in ourselves, look deeply and honestly at yourself during this exercise.

Use the default position approaches as a guide. If some of your reactions to others differed from the list, simply list those reactions as well.

- Use of Power
- Manipulation
- Force of Reason
- Ignore It
- Play Off Relationships
- Make Deals
- Kill the Messenger
- Give In Too Soon

> *I think I used them all at one time or another. But a few stand out. After trying to reason with my staff, I resorted to power to make them implement the plans. Often I made my senior managers my henchmen for this task. . . .*
>
> *With the other hospitals, I used force of reason. I believed that if I was prepared, people would need to agree with me, since the merger was in their best interests. It never worked. I talked and talked and talked. I seldom listened. . . .*
>
> *Just before Hospital C left, I found myself working clandestinely with the CEO of Hospital A as we tried to find ways to get the administrator of Hospital C to agree to our strategies.*

### 5. What Was the Impact?

What was the impact of each of these styles? Did they hinder or help build lasting support for the change?

- What was the immediate impact?
- What was the long-term impact?

List your response as specifically as possible. It is one thing to say that trust declined, but more helpful to list the behavior you actually observed.

> *The short-term impact was that the merger, as first envisioned, failed. Hospital C dropped out. Hospital A told us that they needed time to consider their options. . . .*
>
> *In the long term, it may still be possible to build an alliance with Hospital A and the nursing home. . . .*

*The impact on our staff is harder to measure. I fear that we have destroyed a bond of trust with them. We inflicted the merger on them and demanded that they implement it—and then killed the merger just as quickly. Morale seems lower. Absenteeism is a little higher and turnover is up 10 percent. This may be a fluke, but it's worth noting.*

### 6. Did You Avoid Engaging Those Who Resisted?

Embracing resistance is difficult, and we may avoid it for a number of very good reasons. It is important to recognize that normal, well-intentioned people have difficulty engaging those who resist them. Here are some of the major reasons we fail to embrace resistance.

- **TIME.** The most commonly stated reason for avoiding resistance is time. Like the Mad Hatter, we are late for very important dates. No time to say hello, goodbye, we're late, we're late, we're late. The pace of change is getting even worse. We will have even less time to say hello, goodbye.

   This frantic pace often causes us to work against what we know we should do. Studies indicate that people in organizations do a poor job of communicating on routine matters; no wonder we don't take time to communicate when the issue is resistance.

- **THEY DON'T UNDERSTAND.** We tend to believe that our view of the world is the correct one. When others see things differently, it's easy to dismiss them. Not only don't they understand, but we believe they can't or won't even try to understand. If we are busy, the stench of quarterly reports breathing down our necks, we might be tempted to think, Why waste time on people who can't be saved?

- **FEAR OF LOSS OF CONTROL.** While time and "They don't understand" are certainly legitimate reasons for keeping distance from those who resist us, they pale in comparison to the importance we place on staying in control.

   Most of us want to be in control. We want to know what to expect. We want some degree of predictability even in the midst of change. We want to keep whatever power we now enjoy. When we embrace resistance, we run the risk of bursting open the flood gates and watching the torrent wash away all the familiar landmarks.

   Most would rather stay high above those raging currents. Those who do invite resistance may abandon their goal at the first sounds of rushing water. It takes tremendous faith to enter those waters as a possible tidal wave approaches.

Not making time, failure to take the others seriously, and fear that we will lose control inhibit our ability to make contact with others. They put barriers between us. If we must stay in control, we cannot engage in any dialogue that threatens our position. An honest exchange might reveal that our view is ill-informed. And if we need to stay in control, then we cannot afford to gamble on letting new information in.

*I never truly engaged those who resisted. I blamed it on time, but the truth is that I believed the alliance was the right idea at the right time, and that those who questioned any aspect of it were wrong.*

*I was not able to slow down enough to listen and be influenced by anyone. To do that would have meant relinquishing control.*

*I guess I believed that, if I listened to their complaints, we would get so bogged down that we would never pull off the merger.*

### 7. *What Were Your Patterns?*

Begin to search for patterns in how you reacted. What patterns did you notice?

- Internal reactions?
  - thoughts
  - feelings
  - physical

- External reactions? Which of the common approaches did you use most often?

- Subtle differences, depending on who you were working with? For example, you may have reacted differently to a boss, peers, staff, spouse, children, constituents, and so forth.

*I used force of reason with peers and reverted to power with those who reported to me. That doesn't make for a very pretty picture. I used manipulation with everyone, although I always did it with the best of intentions. I was just trying to find ways to get others to buy in: "What will it take to get the head of nursing to agree to this?"*

These patterns are important. They are your personal default positions. They are reactions and styles you will probably rely on during other changes. Equally important is that your way of responding to resistance may actually invite resistance. For example, people with a confrontational in-your-face style tend to attract conflict. Note the impact your pattern has on how others respond. Managers who hold information close, allowing only a few insiders to know the secret plans, create cultures in which people don't deal directly with each other. The office becomes a breeding ground for Level 2 resistance.

### 8. If You Were to Do It Again...
Imagine you could rewind the tape and start over. What would you do differently? Here are some things to consider. Would you

- involve others earlier?
- involve more groups and individuals in the change?
- use the touchstones?
  - Maintain Clear Focus
  - Embrace Resistance
  - Respect Those Who Resist
  - Relax
  - Join with the Resistance

Think about what you could have done. The intent of this exercise is to learn from experience in order to meet the future with more skills—not to beat yourself or assign blame for past failures.

> *If I could rewind the tape, I would begin in the same way. I needed to check my assumptions with my executive team and make sure they were with me. Our initial meetings with the other facilities were fine.*
>
> *After that I would do a number of things differently. I would invite all the heads of the facilities to join me in creating a vision statement. This statement would describe the dream and how we pictured working together as an alliance. I would make sure that people could get issues out on the table for full discussion.*
>
> *I would suggest that someone else facilitate the meeting to keep me from talking so much. I would question Hospital C when it asked to join us. We accepted them without much discussion. What were they looking for? Were we a good match? Could they provide what we need in our alliance? This might save us the embarrassment of a very public split. . . .*
>
> *As soon as all the parties agreed to form the alliance, I would announce the decision to our staff. I would find ways to get our hospi-*

## THE UNSPOKEN GAME
## AN INTERVIEW WITH GEOFFREY BELLMAN

*Geoffrey Bellman is a consultant and author of* The Consultant's Calling *and* Getting Things Done When You Are Not in Charge. *I am impressed by his willingness to look inward and his candor in expressing what he finds. Even though he speaks about his unique role as a consultant or change agent, I think you'll find his words speak to all who work inside organizations.*

**RM:** Where does resistance come from?

**GB:** It doesn't have to do what's present here in this system. It has to do with the games we are playing in our lives—what we need to be in our own lives. Change agents have defined ourselves as being different from the systems we work in. We have a great resistance to "getting in bed with them," talking like them, losing our specialness. We are afraid we'll be just like them, that we won't be "special" in the ways that we've defined it. Our supposed specialness springs from a little bit of a hierarchical thinking: I'm better, they're worse. Listen to how we talk about the people we work with. At the base of it we're all a bunch of naked human beings. Down underneath it all, in the game we never talk about—the primary game— we're all down there reaching, grasping, clinging, lifting, floating through life. And that's what we have in common—when we take off all the armor—with the organizations we work in. But we seldom acknowledge this. We're all equal in that regard. We all share a resistance to looking into the deeper meaning of what we are doing. We all resist looking deeply into why we are

*tal staff involved in planning for the merger. Perhaps we could set up joint committees with the other facilities. . . .*

*I would make the executive team and myself available to listen to concerns and answer questions openly. . . .*

*When the newspaper story came out on downsizing in the industry, I would respond to it immediately, giving my best guess as to its applicability to our hospital. I would say: If the merger were successful, we would be healthier and probably be able to keep all staff.*

doing what we are doing. And at the same time, we resist letting go of those reasons.

**RM:** So what can help us begin to understand that unspoken game we are each playing?

**GB:** Let go of the idea that we are ever going to fully understand it, but always keep trying to understand the unspoken game. We are always going to be discovering more about ourselves, our games. We need to acknowledge that the game goes beyond our ability to make sense of it. It is a fascinating life mystery. I know this sounds impractical, but it is practical as hell. Another point: Whenever I tell clients to "Do this," "Don't do that," I imply that the game is "solvable." It is not. My advice, my techniques, tools, and mod-

els are only attempts at fuller understanding; these tools will not give me answers, the complete picture. I need to remind myself of that; I need to remind my clients of that.

**RM:** Since we so much want to be in control of situations, this sounds very difficult.

**GB:** Yes. But the tools are just tools, though they do help us find our deeper meaning. But if I can approach the new discoveries about myself with a positive "exploring the mystery" perspective, then new discoveries become new openings. Any personal game becomes much richer than I ever imagined. Richness and frustration seem to go hand in hand, but staying in the searching mode allows me to accept the game as it is.

### 9. Doing It Right

If you completed the first eight questions of the assessment, you may be feeling a bit down. That's a lot of analysis of things that didn't work. To build skills in handling resistance to change, you must know what's not working. However, it is equally important to identify what you have done correctly. This is not just to make you feel good—it's easier to build on what you already do well, to learn why you were successful. What were the conditions? How can you create or expand those conditions to increase your success in the future?[2]

Identify some instances when you have used strategies that honored the touchstones.

*Last year we reengineered, if that's the word, our billing procedures. Just about everyone knew that the old process was an odd combination of various automated and manual systems. It was a costly mess.*

### MAINTAIN CLEAR FOCUS

*I was clear on the goal and committed to seeing it through. I would be personally as involved as I needed to be to make it work. I was delighted that I did not run the project. I called together representatives from across the hospital and asked them to make it happen. We set a date and they began.*

### EMBRACE RESISTANCE

*Some of the people in billing were resisting this "snooping around" by the committee. I met with them. By shutting up and listening, I learned that they felt they were being criticized for doing poor work. I asked more questions and found that they were afraid this might result in a reduction in the work force. I assured them that they were doing good work, and that if the committee recommended less staff, I would do everything I could to redeploy them. And if there were a reduction in force, people would be given plenty of notice and support in finding another job. People weren't happy with this, but they started cooperating with the committee.*

### RESPECT THOSE WHO RESIST

*I listened to them; usually I'm in send mode. I recall one staff member coming up to me afterward and thanking me for the meeting. I can't remember the last time that happened.*

### RELAX

*Before my meeting, I did a dry run with the billing staff, anticipating their questions. This helped me stay calm and I responded more openly during the meeting.*

### JOIN WITH THE RESISTANCE

*At the end of the meeting, I asked for the billing staff's help in this process. And I asked them what they wanted from it as well. They wanted to influence the final process and to be involved in the analysis of the work flow. I agreed. They were right. Their input was invaluable.*

## THE KEY QUESTIONS

If you took the time to complete the assessment, you should have a much better understanding of how you have dealt with resistance in the past. Now, shift focus to the change you are engaged in today. Ask yourself

- Where am I likely to get into trouble?

- What skills that I have already proven I know how to use can I employ to build support for the change?

- Can I see the potential down side of this change? Do I know how I will work with the unexpected? (All changes have unintended consequences, and most leaders of change fail to see them.)

## ALMOST TIME TO ENGAGE

At this point, you should have determined where you are on the cycle, made an educated guess about the intensity of the resistance, and assessed your own reactions to the resistance. You must see where the others are on the cycle, determine how deep their resistance truly is, and begin to put the touchstones to use.

You've done all this in the privacy of your own office. Now it's time to engage those other people and learn about what's really going on.

# PART III
## *Take Action*

# 10 CREATE THE SHIFT

A great many people think they are thinking
when they are merely rearranging their prejudices.
—*William James*

J oining with the Resistance is everything. The goal is to find ways to transform opposing viewpoints into a single common picture. All other touchstones are in service of this single ultimate touchstone— Joining with the Resistance. When you Join, you see the same situation from a fresh perspective. You begin to see possibilities.

## THE SHIFT

Kathie Dannemiller heads Dannemiller-Tyson, a consulting firm that specializes in helping organizations implement major changes. When Ford Motor Company wanted to begin building the new Mustang, they called her group in to assist. Here is how she describes the shift that took place when virtually all management and staff of the Dearborn plant—some 2,400 people—attended the conference.[1]

It was on the third day and we had pulled everyone together to hear from the skunk works group.[2] I asked the plant manager and the union president to each give a fifteen-minute "I have a dream" speech. "I have a dream for a Dearborn assembly plant that. . . ." The plant manager spoke first. At the end of the union president's speech, the plant manager said, "Al, we have the same dream! Let's do it together." They shook hands and then hugged. The whole room erupted in cheers.

As we all walked back to the breakout rooms, I had the illusion that I was walking on air. I looked around and suddenly realized that there was hope.

That's the shift. People could say, "No big deal. We can do this." These people believed that someone cared about them and cared about their plant."[3]

When plant managers and United Auto Workers leaders hug, something is going on. This was not business as usual. A shift had taken place. Neither side has given up anything. The two leaders still had to answer to their constituents, but a shift had occurred that allowed them to see that they held similar dreams.

### Shared Dissatisfaction
Richard Beckhard created a simple equation that shows the relationship between planning and resistance.[4] This is a slight variation on his original model.

$$\frac{\text{Dissatisfaction} \times \text{Vision} \times \text{First Steps}}{\text{Resistance}} = \text{Successful Change}$$

In order for change to be successful, there must be enough shared dissatisfaction with the status quo, a vision of how to proceed, and knowledge of the first steps for moving ahead. Since it is an equation that reads dissatisfaction *times* vision *times* first steps, if any of these factors is at zero, the entire top line becomes zero, and resistance takes over.

Shared dissatisfaction is the most important part of this equation in creating the shift. People will not (and have no reason to) shift if they aren't dissatisfied with the status quo. In terms of the cycle, when people are in the Random Incidents stage they see no need to change.

You must find ways to create shared dissatisfaction. Goals and plans can come later. You are looking for

- common fears
- common hopes
- a common picture of the situation

The shift occurs not so much when people see *your* picture of reality but when your pictures join—when you can say, "Al, we have the same dream. Let's do it together."

## WHAT CREATES A SHIFT?

If potential resistance is fairly mild (Level 1), then information may be all that people need. Like the old commercial, people slap their heads and say, "I could have had a V-8." Once you explain things, others can see possibilities.

However, if the resistance is deeper, information alone will never be enough to create the shift. In fact, information alone will soon turn into the ineffective default strategy Force of Reason, in which, by brute persuasion, you try to make people see that your picture of the situation is the correct one. It doesn't work.

In war, we tend to dehumanize the enemy. We do the same thing in organizations. We do it to protect ourselves. We want to be assured that we are on the side of right and goodness. One purpose of the shift is to make ourselves human once again in each other's eyes. (This is precisely what the Common Ground Network for Life and Choice does when it gets pro-life and pro-choice people talking to each other.)

Unfortunately, you cannot make the shift occur—you can only create conditions that allow it to happen. Here are a few ways that can help.

### *Tell Our Stories*

There is tremendous power in stories. It is difficult to take exception to someone's personal story. As you listen, you have an opportunity to learn about other people. You hear at a deeper level.

Senior management of a hospital were facing difficulty implementing a restructuring that focused on the patient rather than on departmental alliances. An argument ensued when some suggested that maintenance workers be allowed to fill patients' minor requests. They suggested, for example, that if a maintenance worker were in the room and a patient requested a bed pan, the worker should be allowed to get it. Critics countered that only a nurse should be allowed to do this. Patients would be concerned about the sanitary conditions—who knew where the workers' hands had been?

The debate went on, with both sides presenting rational arguments. Then a maintenance worker got up and said, "Do you know how it feels to have a patient ask you for a bedpan and all you can do is say, 'I'll get a nurse for you'? I feel degraded, like I'm not worth anything. I can't even be trusted to get someone a bedpan."[5] He talked from his heart, and others listened. According to the hospital administrator, that simple but heartfelt statement was the turning point in the process.

This man's story touched people at a level that no flowchart or rational argument could ever reach. He spoke to a need shared by all, the need for dignity. His story transformed people's perspectives.

### Self-Disclosure

A variation on telling stories is sharing your accomplishments and failures. The late Ron Lippitt used a very simple technique for getting people to talk about what really mattered. He asked departments (or groups of workers) to identify what they were proud of and what they were sorry about. No one was allowed to critique these self-reports or to comment on someone else's list. People simply listened and took in what their colleagues were saying.

Because it works, this technique is used in many of the organizational change models described in the following chapters. The words "proud" and "sorry" speak to us as humans; they ask that we reveal something of ourselves. We learn something about ourselves and are often surprised to learn that colleagues down the hall really do understand the impact their actions have had on others. We become a bit closer as a result.

### Individual Visions

It is important to hear about people's hopes and dreams. In the early '80s, Borg-Warner, a maker of transmissions and other auto parts, was trying to find ways to improve quality. Management and union would meet to try to make some headway, but everything seemed to fail. (In terms of the cycle, they attempted to Implement things without first seeing whether they had a shared Recognition of the issues.)

During one of these meetings, someone suggested that everyone write his or her vision for the company on a large sheet of paper and that these be posted, unsigned, around the room. Once all the sheets were posted, a shift occurred. Management and labor alike realized that they could not tell who had written which statement. It was impossible to tell management's and labor's visions apart. At that moment they realized they could work together on this challenge. They soon improved quality so much that Borg-Warner was awarded Ford's coveted preferred-supplier status, Q-1.[6]

Our visions are our hopes. I find clients amazed by the visions of their colleagues, at how often their visions align in deep and important ways. You can almost hear them saying as they listen, "I didn't know they felt that way."

### Shared Meaning

All of these ideas add to the common database. As we learn more about each other—our yearnings and fears, our accomplishments and failures—we begin to see that we are in this together.

## IN SEARCH OF A SHIFT

In chapter 7, Where Are You Today?, I discussed three possible placements on the cycle: Way Out Ahead, In It Together, and Stalled. Knowing where you are on the cycle will help you formulate strategies that can allow a shift to occur.

### In It Together

Just because you are at the beginning of an effort doesn't mean that there isn't resistance. Recall all the factors listed in chapter 8, How Intense Is the Resistance?, that could have an impact on this change—issues such as the history of change, outside forces, bureaucratic culture, and level of cooperation in the past. Even when everyone is starting together, it is still important to learn how to unleash and explore the resistance.

I suggest one change for the Beckhard equation: I would add "Sensitivity to Potential Resistance."

$$\frac{\text{Dissatisfaction} \times \text{Vision} \times \text{First Steps} \times \underline{\text{Sensitivity to Potential Resistance}}}{\text{Resistance}} = \text{Successful Change}$$

Even after you've experienced a shift, resistance may still develop. A shift is a major breakthrough. It signals that those who must support you have said that they are with you—and that you are with them. But the cycle has just begun its circuit. Many things can happen along the way. A change in management could disrupt movement, or a misunderstood directive could rekindle old fears. You must keep your antennae out ready to pick up signs of an approaching storm.

The next chapter describes a number of ways to work collaboratively with other individuals and groups to create a shared vision.

### Way Out Ahead

The ideas presented in the next chapter will also work if you are Way Out Ahead, but you must be willing to slow down so that others can join you. And you must be willing to be influenced by what they have to say.

If you are Way Out Ahead, resistance may already have descended to deeper levels. You must get at the nature of the resistance before you can make progress.

### *Stalled*

Borg-Warner's early efforts in cooperation stalled. It was only when they backed up that they were able to find the common vision. It was then that the shift occurred that told them they were In It Together. Some of the ideas listed in this chapter may be especially helpful in unsticking the cycle.

# 11 PREEMPT RESISTANCE

The lions might lie down with the lambs,
but the lambs won't get much sleep.
—*Woody Allen*

The makers of Fram oil filters ran a popular commercial in which a mechanic wiped grease from his hands, nodded toward a car on the lift, and said, "You can pay me now or you can pay me later."

You must attend to resistance. You can either work with it now, when the cycle is young and you are all exploring the world of possibilities, or you can pay later, when resistance is firmly entrenched. You have that choice.

You need to find strategies that increase the opportunities for contact among individuals and groups. Even when the change is young, it is important to find ways to create a shift from independent ideas into a single vision, with all aligned. Obviously, it is easiest to create that shift during the early stages of a change, before animosities have had a chance to build and before the wall is built.

In this chapter I explore some alternatives that can begin to build support for change. But first, it is important to examine the nature of trust.

## THE DILEMMA OF TRUST

Trust building is like preventive medicine. It creates a corporate immune system that can handle the stress of change. When the corporate body is healthy, it can handle disruption with far greater ease.

Trust suggests that you share some sense of common purpose, some mutual interests, values, and dreams; with regard to your shared goals, you trust that the other individual or group will act in your best interests as well as their own. The answers to "What's in it for me?" and "What's in it for them?" may not be the same, but they do complement each other. As trust increases, common ground develops. On this firm soil you can create strong foundations.

The dilemma is that trust is difficult to build and easy to destroy. Yet it is essential if you ever hope to build long-lasting support and commitment for your ideas. Leaders of organizations often fail to pay attention to building trust and then are surprised when people grow suspicious of their motives.

Spending time building support for your ideas in the early stages of the cycle may seem a waste of time. Competitors are breathing down your neck, stockholders are uneasy; you feel you must take action quickly. Your instincts are probably right; but that initial action should be to build trust.

Think of it this way: Change is not likely to diminish during your lifetime. As Herodotus wrote centuries ago, change is the only constant—and it hasn't gotten any better since the fall of Athens. You can go from change to change gracelessly and off balance, making enemies and seeing resistance destroy your plans, or you can take the time to build a base that reduces deeper levels of resistance. If people trust you, then most resistance you face will be Level 1. People might question the wisdom of an idea, ask for more input, wonder about strategies or priorities—but their resistance will be based on their concern over the project. Their spoken resistance won't mask a deeper level. What you see is what you get.

### The Opposite of Trust Is Fear

Jack Gibb suggested that the absence of trust is not benign passivity but a more active force: fear.[1] The greater the fear, the stronger the resistance. Fear is an incubator for the malignant growth of resistance. As we get into projects and find ourselves pushing ahead of others on the cycle, we increase fear. Resistance deepens, and we become polarized.

The "Off with their heads!" approach to corporate downsizing, one of many fear-inducing strategies, seldom works. Senior management assumes that once the cuts are made, those remaining will hunker down and efficiency will improve. Often, the opposite occurs. The survivors fear that they may be next and begin to see every management action as a sign that the axe will fall again. Senior management have driven a wedge between themselves and staff, rending the fragile strands of trust. Senior management then wonder why people aren't getting on board.[2]

### Push for Honesty

Trust is built as people take risks and talk honestly to one another. The dilemma, of course, is that if you wait for others to show their colors, they will probably wait for you to do the same. It will be a long wait. Trust comes from doing the things that engender trust. Pushing for honesty can help this.

We both love and hate honest communication. On the one hand we know that it is the best policy and gets critical issues on the table; on the other, it destroys our little fantasy bubbles about who we are. Movie mogul Samuel Goldwyn expressed this dilemma well when he said, "I want people to tell me the truth, even if it costs them their jobs."

Even with our ambivalence about honesty, we must push ahead. We cannot build trust or commitment to change without it.

### Trust, But Verify

During nuclear arms reduction talks between the Soviet Union and the United States, "Trust, but verify" became an important principle for negotiators. Both sides had sufficient trust to sit down at the table together, but enough sense to know that they needed a safety net. Neither side could afford to trust blindly. They needed ways to verify that promises made would be promises kept. Often we want others to trust us just because we say we are trustworthy. Richard Nixon's "I am not a crook" was a much-parodied remark. He seemed not to understand that he couldn't simply ask for trust, but had to earn it.

When working with others where trust is low, you must offer ways they can verify what they are committing to. The director of a division was tired of people trying to tell him how to run his shop. In spite of a history of mistrust in which others in the organization felt that his department had not been responsive, he wanted them to trust him. He pleaded with them to give him a chance, but offered nothing in return. People were reluctant to turn over full control to him.

He could have built support for himself and his department if he had only acknowledged what everyone knew was true, asked what they needed from him, and then developed a plan to show how he intended to accomplish these goals—

and given them a way to monitor progress. He just repeated the tired refrain, Trust me. They didn't.

The interesting paradox was that the more he demanded their trust, the deeper their suspicion grew.

## "WHAT IF?" SCENARIOS

Often the depth of the resistance doesn't even become apparent to us until we are asked to take action. For example, an administrative unit within a government agency was considering ways to improve efficiency. Their customers began to demand faster response time. The department's manual systems were no match for a clientele used to the speed of fax and modem communications. Although they faced resistance during the early stages of planning, it wasn't until the group began suggesting specific strategies that the deepest resistance surfaced. People who had supported the early planning became suspicious of the very strategies they had been supporting. It was not that they had been holding out, waiting for the right time to disrupt progress, it was just that as they got closer to implementing plans, they discovered factors they felt they had to resist.

The U.S. Army Corp of Engineers developed a method to get issues out on the table before they become conflicts.[3] All players involved in a construction project come together to define what this temporary partnership will look like. They discuss how they will handle such issues as quality, completion dates, costs and cost overruns, safety, and paperwork.

They address things that could go wrong. This is a pretty easy task; everyone in the business knows where the hassles are. Then they devise strategies for dealing with these potential pitfalls. Think of these as "What If?" scenarios.

Exploring what might happen is much safer than trying to tackle a problem when it is facing you. "What If?" scenarios allow you to step back and calmly play with possibilities without the risk.

Here are some things to consider:

1. If the groups have worked together before, identify projects where the groups were in conflict. If the groups are new, ask people to draw on their own experience to identify potential conflict over the change.

   Do not assign blame. The goal is to identify issues that could come up during the current change, not dissect the particular past events.

2. Form mixed groups with representatives from a cross section of departments and levels of the organizations involved. Have those groups take

on the issues identified in Step 1 and develop strategies to address these problems should they occur.

Consider the five touchstones as you develop strategies. Groups should address the following questions:

- How can we keep our focus on the goal if this issue occurs? (Maintain Clear Focus)

- How will we summon the courage to stick with it, even if the going gets extremely tough? (Maintain Clear Focus)

- What can we do to ensure mutual respect in the midst of this issue? (Respect)

- What can we do to ensure that all the critical issues get out on the table? (Embrace Resistance)

- How can we stay relaxed in the midst of this conflict? (Relax)

- How can we promote the development of common values? (Join with the Resistance)

3. Subgroups report to the full group all questions, comments, and suggested changes.

4. The full group decides which of these strategies it can fully support.

## REAL TIME STRATEGIC CHANGE

Kathie Dannemiller and her associates at Dannemiller-Tyson developed an effective model called Real Time Strategic Change that allows people to influence an existing vision and revise a strawman plan.[4] (I referred to this briefly in the previous chapter.) Here's how it works:

The typical first step is for senior management to bring all key stakeholders together. These highly structured meetings often involve a few hundred people. During the conference, speakers present background information to help increase recognition of the need for the change. They may call in experts as well as representatives from similar organizations to speak to the group.

People are placed at tables in "maxmix" (maximum mixture) groups. Each table represents a cross section of the organization. (Of course, people never sit with their bosses.) This almost guarantees fertile discussion as representatives from across the organization tackle critical problems.

A presentation is followed by questions and answers. For example, suppose someone has just presented the reasons the organization must improve its distribution system. Each maxmix table would discuss three questions:

- What did we hear?
- What were our reactions?
- What questions of understanding do we have?

Some tables would be called on to ask their questions of clarification. Speakers at the front table would respond.

The same format is followed when the proposal for change is offered. In Real Time Strategic Change, senior management presents a clear proposal for action. In terms of the cycle of change, they offer a model that describes how the change would be integrated into the organization.

Making a strong statement is like pumping adrenaline into the meeting. People react. Some may love it. Some may hate it. Others may scratch their heads. But few are slack jawed and uninterested.

The maxmix process allows people to voice their concerns. Since maxmix groups foster diversity of thought, presentations to the full group create a sense of common ground and direction.

Senior management or the planning team often meet late into the night to revise their plan based on what they have heard. The next day they propose the revisions to the group, and the dialogue continues. Depending on the goals of the Real Time Strategic Change sessions, it is possible to move an organization from Random Incidents to the beginning of Implementation in a matter of days.

## FUTURE SEARCH

Marvin Weisbord, building on the search conferences of Fred and Merrilyn Emery and on Ron Lippitt and Eva Schindler-Rainman's futures conferences, created his own version of a conference that would build common ground and vision.[5] During a Future Search conference, representatives from all key stakeholder groups gather to discuss the future of the organization. (Weisbord suggests a maximum of seventy people.) Before discussing the future, participants examine the past and the current situations. In a typical conference, large sheets of paper might be placed on the walls indicating three periods, say 1965–75, 1976–86, and 1987–1997, with each sheet divided into three parts—personal reflections, organizational history, and the larger world. Participants write their recollections of significant events in each of these areas over the past thirty years. In the process, people rub shoulders, chat, and of course read what others have written.

After the writing ends, people begin to look at themes within each category and trends that continue from decade to decade. More experienced staff recall the history of the organization and the pressures they faced over the years. Newer staff learn about critical events that occurred before they arrived. People begin to see that they are all in this together. They often realize that they share considerable common ground. All begin to see the trends that may shape their future.

Later, people divide into their respective groups within the organization to identify their "proudest prouds" and "sorriest sorries." They present these lists to the full group. Self-disclosure is a key factor in building trust. When a department admits that it has been less than responsive over the years, some are relieved, while others are often surprised that the department seems to understand the impact it has had on the rest of the organization.

Future Search continues with many other activities that build a common understanding of the organization. Based on this knowledge, people meet in mixed groups to develop visions for a preferred future.

Future Search addresses the need to build a common base before proceeding around the change cycle. It lets all move along the cycle together. Future Search can take an organization from Random Incidents through Recognition to Initial Actions.

A typical Future Search lasts three days. Compared with the difficulty many organizations have in making any progress at all along the cycle, moving from Random Incidents to Initial Actions in that short a time may seem a miracle. The secret, of course, is that this technique builds trust first. Taking time to build the foundation allows future activities to move much more quickly.

## STRUCTURED DIALOGUE

One of the most difficult aspects of building trust (or dealing with resistance) is accepting the fact that other sane and right-minded people may see the world differently than you. Hard to believe, isn't it?

The Common Ground Network for Life and Choice uses an interesting exercise to get people to begin a dialogue on abortion.[6] They ask people to tell their stories—how they came to believe what they believe. Think about it. How can we argue with other people's stories? We can argue with their viewpoints, but not with their stories.

Often these stories begin to dissolve barriers. People begin to see the person behind the position. Hearing another's story helps us see the world from her vantage point. Although we may have made different choices, we begin to see why she made the choices she did.

Here are some things that make this approach work.

### Joint Planning

Both sides have to agree not only to take part but to help organize the event. The planners (not the Common Ground Network) create goals for the meeting and select facilitators.

### Ground Rules

People must agree to abide by certain rules of conduct in the meeting:

- Speak for yourself.
- Maintain confidentiality (some people are willing to take part but don't want others to know they were at the session).
- Do not make inflammatory comments.
- Do not attempt to convert others.
- Respect others.

These ground rules tell people it will be safe to speak. They create a boundary, a DMZ, where it is safe to walk.

### Start Easy

People need to feel safe in the meeting. They begin with such simple questions as, What are the risks in being here today? This is not an insignificant question, but it is fairly easy to address. As opposed to a silly get-acquainted icebreaker, this question gets people talking personally right away.

Subsequent questions get more difficult: What is the heart of the issue for you? What's a question you've always wanted to ask the other group? (This exchange would take place only after groups had shown they could listen to and respect each other.)

### Room to Talk

People meet in groups of four (two pro-choice, two pro-life) with a facilitator to discuss issues. This ensures that people get a chance to talk. Larger groups run the risk of having a few dominant people take over.

### Room to Explore

Goals for the initial meetings ("workshops") are usually framed as opportunities to explore the issues. The Common Ground Network wisely avoids suggesting too quickly that these dialogues turn into action planning. When that occurs, it is too easy for people to begin trying to sell their plans. This builds walls, not common ground.

I believe that one of the most powerful aspects of all these organizational change models is actually quite simple: they bring people together who may never have had occasion to talk to one another. By working together, they begin to see that those other people are just as dedicated and concerned about the issues facing the organization as they are. They become human in each other's eyes.

## ROLL YOUR OWN

As much as I like "What If?" scenarios, Real Time Strategic Change, Future Search, and Structured Dialogue, I include them only to demonstrate what is possible. There are many other ways to build support from the beginning. Washington Gas, the provider of natural gas to the Washington, D.C., metropolitan area, has some 725,000 customers.[7] Management doesn't get many complaints, but it takes seriously those it does receive. The former president received some one hundred letters a year from unhappy customers. Since each undoubtedly represented many people who never got around to writing, he realized that even a single letter was one too many. He decided to act.

In the summer of 1994, a group was assigned to look for common themes in the letters. It found four major opportunities for improvement: concern for the customer's problem, helpfulness in finding a solution, knowledge of the issue, and courtesy.

Senior vice presidents Pat Clark and James DeGraffenreidt (who is now president) decided on a unique approach to tackling these issues. They wanted everyone who dealt directly with customers to be involved in suggesting solutions, and they wanted quick results. High involvement and rapid implementation often work at cross purposes, so they needed something that would get everyone's input and creative suggestions quickly. The president wanted immediate results.

Working with Jan Chapman they created a process in Washington Gas's Quality Department almost overnight. Over a two-week period, some three hundred people met in groups of twenty to thirty, two to three hours per group, to examine the four themes.

Since almost everyone had received training in quality improvement, they used a common six-step problem-solving process that most people in the company understood:

1. Identify and select the problem.
2. Analyze the problem.
3. Generate potential solutions.
4. Select and plan the solution.
5. Implement the solution.
6. Evaluate the solution.

The first group met with one of the senior vice presidents (either DeGraffenreidt or Clark attended each session) to discuss step 1. Each subsequent group picked up where the last group left off. For example, a group might have focused on generating solutions. The facilitators met between sessions to see whether they needed to explore the step further. If the answer were yes, the next group of fifteen examined another aspect of generating solutions. By the end of the two weeks, everyone had worked through the entire process.

I like this approach for a several reasons. It is fast and simple to execute, gets everyone into the act, and is inexpensive. Here are some of the reasons why I believe it worked so well at Washington Gas.

### Clear Customer Information

The company based the process on real customer issues. There was nothing theoretical about this exercise. Everyone knew that these were issues that had to be addressed because customers told them so.

### A Way to Measure

The company already had processes in place to measure these four areas, so monitoring progress would be easy. Measurement was important. It would let them know whether their ideas worked as well in practice as they did during brainstorming.

### Everyone Involved

People are more likely to accept changes they had a hand in creating, and people closest to the customer see the problems and opportunities far more clearly than others.

### Communication to All

After each day, everyone was sent a summary of the day's activities. Even if people had already been in a session, they could respond to the summary, and this input would be given to the next group. Thus, each person could influence the outcome throughout the planning period.

### Top Management Actively Involved

DeGraffenreidt and Clark wisely chose to make sure one or the other of them attended all the sessions. They believed it was important for people to see that senior management took the work seriously.

### They Were Willing to Be Influenced

Senior management entered the project hoping that people would focus on things they could personally change. Although staff did make many suggestions that met that goal, they also suggested restructuring credit and collection as well as the customer-service arm. The two SVPs wisely listened to those issues as well and approved some restructuring.

## THE FOUNDATION

In order to build trust in the beginning, you still need to attend to the touch-stones. I include a number of different ways to build support for the change and build trust at the same time. All honor the touchstones.

### MAINTAIN CLEAR FOCUS

Each model presents a clear goal for the meeting or conference. People come together for a specific purpose. Other, unrelated, issues are not addressed.

### EMBRACE RESISTANCE

All the models allow people to express their concerns, and since these sessions are short on presentation and high on involvement, people have an opportunity to wrestle with issues.

### RESPECT THOSE WHO RESIST

Just inviting all the stakeholders shows respect. All the designs are built around active participation. All voices are important. The for-mats allow people to be heard.

### RELAX

The structures provide security. Although it might seem that work-ing with large groups could become chaotic—the lynch-mob phe-nomenon—the designs are so highly organized that it allows people to feel safe. Bad things usually don't happen.

### JOIN WITH THE RESISTANCE

All parties seek a common ground that includes the goals of all the groups.

---

### *Fast Action*

Senior management were looking for things they could fix quickly. Many of the solutions were implemented within days after the final session. Seventy percent of the suggestions were implemented within the first few months. In addition to the quick-fix solutions, the company began longer-range activities, such as restructuring and developing a new training curriculum. If they had been given plenty of time to complete this process, they might have selected another, less effective, approach. Speed was like an infusion of energy. The process was moving so fast that it simply didn't have a chance to bog down and die of inertia.

### *Flexibility*
Since each session gave the team new data, there was no way of predicting what should be covered in the next session. This demanded that teams remain open to whatever they heard so that they could respond to whatever was needed.

### *Common Frame of Reference*
Since everyone knew the six-step problem-solving model, it provided a common language. Even those who entered the process late could see where their contributions fit.

Although it is too early to tell how effective these changes will be, initial reports are quite promising. People seem committed to the decisions, and preliminary results indicate that customer satisfaction is increasing.

The thing that links all these shift-creating approaches is the value they place on people and their commitment to getting people involved in the process as early as possible. There is no reason why we can't invent our own models. The field is young. These are times of experimentation. We are just learning about ways to cooperate in large, complex organizations.

# 12 UNLEASH ITS POWER

Ye shall know the truth,
and the truth shall make you mad.
—*Aldous Huxley*

Five days before its massive eruption in 1980, Mount Saint Helens simmered and smoked as pressure built inside. Everyone knew it would blow, but none could predict its power. How high would flames shoot into the Washington sky? How much molten rock would vomit from its mouth—and where would the lava run?

Resistance is a lot like Mount Saint Helens. You can guess, you can make estimates, but you can't tell for certain how strong it will be until it erupts. Polite conversations, hurried executive briefings, lip-service exchanges with staff give only a hint of the pressure that builds deep below the surface.

With good reason, people are frightened of volcanoes. Most residents and visitors clear off the mountain well in advance of the eruption. Getting out of the way of spewing lava makes sense, and that's why the notion of embracing resistance may seem crazy. To deal with resistance effectively you must be willing to summon its fire. You must encourage flames and red-hot ashes to shoot high into the conference room. You cannot be satisfied with whiffs of smoke; you need to feel the rumbling roar of its full force. This chapter focuses on ways to use the touchstone Embrace Resistance.

## WHY UNLEASH RESISTANCE?

There are two reasons for taking this counterintuitive approach. First, you cannot anticipate the extent of resistance until you see it and feel its heat. As long as the mountain looks calm, you don't know what to expect.

If you think of resistance as energy, you can see that the only way to use it productively is to let it surface. Imagine a large generator, capable of transforming fire and heat into electricity, sitting atop Mount Saint Helens. That powerful energy is available to you only when the volcano is erupting.

You need to find ways to unleash resistance safely.

## PICK UP THE SIGNS

Yogi Berra once said, "You can observe a lot just by watching." Once you know what to look for, you begin to see the many faces of resistance. That's the first step. Once you see it, you can address it. Recall the ways to spot it (chapter 2, The Nature of Resistance):

- Confusion
- Quick criticism
- Denial
- Malicious compliance
- Sabotage
- Easy agreement
- Deflection
- Silence
- In-your-face criticism

You may see the silence of the resistance in a meeting, hear a strong-willed rebuttal as you wait for an elevator, or witness the effects of a saboteur. These are data warning you that you are sitting atop a potential volcano.

### *The Grunt*

Employees at a large company were quite angry over management practices. An underground newspaper called *The Grunt* appeared. It was cheap, put together on the sly. It was filled with invective and took devastating swipes at management.

Management began to seek out those responsible for its publication—not to engage them in dialogue and learn about the resistance, but to punish them. If management had acted with courage, they could have learned a lot from *The Grunt*—not so much from the content of the paper, but just from its very existence. The fact that people took the time and risk to write it said a lot about management–labor relations in this company. Unfortunately, senior management's search-and-destroy mission just added to the fear and suspicion.

### Restroom Talk

The signals are sometimes difficult to see and are best picked up outside the official forums—in restrooms, on elevators, over lunch, in hallways, or while perusing your organization's version of *The Grunt*.

A few years ago I was observing a group of managers discussing the challenges and changes facing their organization. The meeting seemed to be going along well. Nothing in their words or actions indicated a problem. It wasn't until we took a break and I ran into one of the players in the men's room that I learned the truth. I asked, "How's the meeting going?" To my surprise, he said, "Same old stuff. We never get anything done." Later I ran into another manager. Her reply was similar. On and on it went—no one thought this was a productive meeting, yet when they met no one ever mentioned dissatisfaction.[1]

### The Dead Thing on the Table

Imagine a dead elephant lying on the table in a conference room.[2] It lies there rotting. Everyone sees it and no one mentions it. People lean and stand to look around and over it—but no one says a word about it. Acknowledging what everyone knows to be true can be a powerful way to begin to get resistance out in the open.

In a staff meeting of engineers, the real issues facing the group were cleverly avoided: no one mentioned the carcass. During a break, tension rose to the breaking point for one team member. When they reconvened, she said, "The problem with us is turf issues. We all feel like we've got to hoard all the resources we can get our hands on. That makes it impossible for us to work together." The dead thing came alive. It was no longer possible to pretend those issues didn't exist. The mere mention of the issue caused sighs of relief—at last they could talk about it.

### INVITE THE STORM

There is no single best way to get resistance out on the table. The approach you take should be based on your personal preferences and your knowledge of what works in your organization.

Years ago, when I first began working as a consultant, I agreed to facilitate a retreat in which management and staff within a state education agency would explore issues impeding their working together. The opening hours of the meeting seemed to go pretty well, but then the wind shifted. Without warning, people started criticizing me—and I was just the facilitator. What was going on?

To deal with their resistance, I drew on the conventional approaches. I reminded them of my role: "I'm not here to take sides. I'm a trained professional" (Force of Reason). They would have none of it. The attacks continued. I tried another tactic—shifting to the next topic on the agenda (Ignore). That didn't work either. They weren't moving. And on it went until, mercifully, the time came for a break.

Fortunately, I had had the good sense to invite Lloyd Richards, one of the most experienced consultants I knew, to join me. During the break, he pulled me aside. "Rick, there is a thunderstorm out there. You didn't create the storm, but since you are the highest point, you are drawing all its electricity. You've got a choice. Either you can continue to stand there like an old tree and take all the hits, or you can be like a lightning rod and allow the electricity to pass through you."

His advice worked. After the break, I used that metaphor and purposely drew even more hits. I copied their questions, concerns, and criticisms on the board. Once the storm had passed and the air had cleared, they were able to examine the issues under calmer skies.

You must invite the storm. Simply listening to the distant thunder won't do. You must be willing to stand atop a hill and bring the storm to you. Here are a number of possibilities to consider.

### Ask Them Directly

After the massive downsizing in the 1980s that earned him the unflattering nickname "Neutron Jack," GE chairman Jack Welch asked those attending the company's Management Institute what the reaction to these changes were out in the field. Managers told him of their deep concerns: people were overwhelmed trying to do the work of those who had gone, and stress was high.

On the helicopter back to corporate headquarters, Welch turned to the institute's director and told him to come up with some way to work out these issues. By inviting people to speak the truth, he heard things that prompted the development of GE's Workout Program. (See the box for a description of the process.)

Workout is a gathering in which the company's employees—sometimes all of them—tell management what they think. It's not easy or fun, but it can put a lot of information on the table quickly. A middle manager described how it worked in one plant. "We were getting screws from one supplier that were not so good. The bits would break off the screw heads, and scratch the product, and cut people's hands—

we had one guy get eighteen stitches. Tempers flared, but management never went and fixed it. They said, 'Okay, we'll go get you some screws from the good supplier.' But then the bad screws would always reappear. So a shop steward named Jimmy stood up at Workout and told the story. This guy was a maverick, a rock thrower, a naysayer. He wanted to test us, to see whether we really wanted to change.

"He knew what he was talking about. And he explained the solution, which had to do with how deep the bit could be inserted into the screw head.

"We listened, then asked, 'Okay, what do you suggest?'

"He replied, 'We need to go tell the supplier what the problems are.'

"Well, I was nervous about it, but I decided to charter a plane to fly Jimmy and a couple other guys to the plant in Virginia where they made the bad screws.

"Jimmy got the problem fixed, and it sent a powerful message to everyone here. He became a leader instead of a maverick, simply because we gave them the forum and allowed him to have some ownership."[3]

A Workout-style meeting can be quite effective if management truly wants to hear the truth. But it takes tremendous fortitude to stand in front of a large room inviting criticism.

---

### WORKOUT

GE's approach to getting issues out on the table and dealing with them is quite simple in design. Its power comes from the safety it offers participants.

1.    People get away from the office or plant and dress casually. The informality and the change of location send a message that this meeting will not be business as usual.

2.    Bosses are kept out of the room during discussions. Facilitators meet with staff to identify issues and make concrete proposals. Often people spend much of the time complaining. This unleashes the resistance and is usually followed by solid ideas.

3.    When managers return, they must make decisions about the proposals publicly and on the spot. Typically 80 percent get immediate yes or no decisions from managers, and decisions must be made on the rest within a month.

# THE POWER OF OPEN INVOLVEMENT
## INTERVIEWS WITH PETER JOHNSON AND JACK ROBERTSON

*Peter Johnson became administrator of Bonneville Power Administration, a federal agency in the Department of Energy, at a time when its reputation and credibility were at an all-time low. With the able counsel of his chief-of-staff, Jack Robertson, he created a model of public involvement that has been studied around the world. Both the pro-environment Natural Resources Defense Council and the Center for Excellence in Government praised BPA for its significant accomplishments in including public participation in government decision making. (See Resources section for more on this story.)*

**RM:** Bonneville Power's Public Involvement Policy is still in effect after all these years. How long did it take to get it adopted?

**PJ:** Two years, because it was such a radical change in the way people had done business. If I had tried to force a public participation policy in six months or mandated it, it would have failed. I had to let people massage it and change it.

**RM:** But initially you viewed the conflict that accompanied involvement as an annoyance.

**PJ:** My entire experience had been in the private sector. I had been a CEO running a very dynamic, very successful company with plants across the United States and Canada. My whole concentration had been on product, R and D, marketing, organization, motivation—all those things that a businessman would concentrate on. I didn't pay a great deal of attention to the environmental community. When I came to Bonneville, suddenly these people were in a position to exert great influence either politically or legislatively. People weren't sure that I understood their point of view and, more than not, I probably didn't.

Historically, Bonneville had generally yielded on many things they shouldn't have yielded on, so we were seen as easy picking if someone chose to bluff us in the courts. My first deputy said that when someone wanted something out of Bonneville, all they had to do was threaten to sue. I put a stop to this approach which had resulted in some poor decisions. Jack Robertson persuaded me there was only one way to deal with these folks who were feeling the impact of what we were doing, and that was to involve them in the decision-making process.

**RM:** What did you do?

**PJ:** I challenged my people and myself to find creative $2 + 2 = 5$ synergistic solutions. Sometimes you find compromise, sometimes you build consensus, but the important thing is that you seek the people who are going to be affected by the decisions you are going to make. You open a process whereby you can communicate with them and understand their points-of-view about the things that are concerning them. At the same time, there's a two-way communication and educational process going on. Believe it or not, you can often find beneficial win-win solutions. Folks are quite satisfied and they like the fact that you listened to them and moved on their ideas. But, if you listened and didn't move, you've got to make sure you explain why you couldn't be more accommodating to their concerns.

Bonneville Power had incredible legal obligations that we had to meet. In the end there were certain things we didn't compromise. Those were communicated to people very clearly and they would respect that. They may not have agreed or been happy with the decision, but they would respect it. They might even openly support it.

**RM:** How do you know when it's OK to move ahead?

**PJ:** You've got to know when you've done everything that would be reasonable under the circumstances to consult with impacted parties and have taken into account their concerns to the highest practical degree. It's a judgment call, because you're never going to get everybody on board. You can't dally or procrastinate and not make a decision. For example, one of the major issues I faced was the settlement of a contentious $2 billion law suit that took a year and a half—that was almost rushing it. It was so bloody complex and there were so many parties to take into account. We had to bring them along to where they could say, "Yes, my concerns have been dealt with." But at the moment it became right, I had

*continued on page 146*

to make a decision to move quickly. Once you've exhausted all your inquiries, you've got to make a clear decision quickly, then enforce it decisively. You gain respect as a decision maker when you do that.

**RM:** So, what advice do you have for others who need to get buy-in for major changes?

**PJ:** We always have to remain self-critical. We have to make sure that what we are doing is the right thing and remain intellectually honest, particularly when our egos get wrapped up in something. So I would say to critically assess your ego and biases and the degree to which they might be causing you to force something where, if you were to think more rationally, you might alter your course or maybe step back and reconsider it entirely.

Listen to those people who will be affected by what you are going to do and involve them creatively. You've got to be your own worst critic in

evaluating your point of view and where you are coming from. But if you are right and come up with something that is really meritorious, and have allowed those you rely on to carry it out to shape it, then you've got to move ahead.

**RM:** Jack, why were you such a strong advocate for public participation?

**JR:** It was clear to me, prior to accepting the job, there had to be radical change. By radical, I mean fundamental and deep, and it had to be a commitment to an openness and involvement with key constituents and decision making or we would not survive as an institution.

**RM:** You mentioned in the *Harvard Business Review* article that you asked Peter for his credit card. What did that mean?

**JR:** I told him, "There's going to be a point where you're going to need to take on faith that what I'm going to tell you is necessary in terms of this fundamental

### Solicit Feedback in Advance

Listening to a room full of people light into you and your pet ideas takes tremendous courage. And it is a very dangerous approach to try. When you hear raw, unfiltered criticism, you may react defensively. I have seen people lash back at those who were telling them truth as they saw it. If you lash back, you make change. It's going to be opposed, it's going to be difficult. There may even be good logic on why you might not want to do this at the time it is proposed, but I'm just telling you there will be a time when I'm going to need your credit card." What I meant by that was that I was going to need him to grant me his authority. I said, "You're going to have to do it to get this change to happen." It turned out he was as good as his word.

**RM:** What did public involvement look like from your perspective at Bonneville?

**JR:** Public involvement is the act of actually interacting and dealing peer to peer. Working across a table with your sleeves rolled up, looking at individuals and groups around the region, and treating them as intellectual equals. Listening to them while never giving up your ultimate responsibility to make a decision. Allowing yourself to be flexible enough to change your mind based on what you hear. If you don't understand what public involvement takes, you should not get into it, because it will be seen as a cynical exercise.

**RM:** How did you deal with other groups in these meetings?

**JR:** It was an interesting dynamic. Peter went into a room with environmentalists who looked like the enemy to many people at Bonneville. Many people just didn't want to deal with them if they could avoid it. Peter talked to them regularly. They could put anything they wanted on table. He took the heat and responded. And he could put whatever he wanted on the table as well. Bonneville Power had become entrenched in its ways, had become arrogant and uncaring, so that when you actually engaged in over-the-fence honest discussion on complex issues it took people's breath away. Those first meetings became legendary. People believed what we said.

matters worse. Once people see that it is unsafe to speak, they quit talking. Try a safer alternative.

A division manager of a financial services company was beginning to hear mounting criticism of some changes he had initiated in service standards. Although most everyone in the organization recognized that they had to stay ahead of the competition in providing the highest quality service, they wondered whether he was serious about the changes. What impact would they have on careers? He asked everyone who had a concern or question to write it anonymously and submit it to him prior to an all-hands meeting so he could look at all the papers before he faced his one-hundred-person management team.

In the meeting, I watched him respond openly to all the questions and comments. Because he seemed to appreciate the questions, others began asking follow-up questions. He had found a safe way to invite and unleash some of the major criticism and concern about his program. Would he hear all of it in a single meeting? Probably not. The eruptions on Mount Saint Helens lasted for weeks. Why should our lives be any easier?

### Make It Easy for People to Speak

Start with the familiar: allow people to talk with others whom they trust. During a particularly painful reorganization, senior management needed to hear what was blocking implementation. It was important for all units to get crucial issues out on the table. People began by discussing these issues in their own groups first. By starting work in familiar surroundings, people gained comfort talking about issues. One person recorded comments and reported the results of the discussion to the entire group. Since comments were not attributed to the individuals who made them, people felt some degree of safety.

Once issues are mentioned publicly, the spell is lifted. People often feel free to address things openly that an hour before were taboo.

### Review Formal Surveys

Anonymous employee surveys can provide a wealth of information if you use resistance as the lens to examine the results. Many companies routinely ask staff to complete one of these attitude surveys. Typically, they include questions about leadership, teamwork, planning—virtually all aspects of management and human relations. Often managers or teams method throughout the organization develop strategies to raise poor scores and keep better practices on track.

In addition to interpreting the results as you normally would, consider what they are saying in light of the proposed (or recently implemented) changes.

- Has trust in management risen or fallen?

- Do people seem surprisingly confused about the direction you are going?

- Do any of the narrative comments pertain to the changes occurring in your organization?

If you see signs of resistance embedded in these results, you must search further. Suppose that confidence in senior management has fallen from 6.2 to 3.1 over the past two years. All this tells you is that the scores have dropped dramatically; you need to learn why. You will undoubtedly make assumptions about the meaning of this decline, but you can't be certain of the meaning until you ask. You must combine these survey results with some other active method of unleashing resistance, for example, a variation on Workout or focus group meetings.

### Informal Questionnaires

You can prepare quick surveys to get instant information regarding the change. A few well-chosen questions can give you vital information.

If you use surveys, you must give people the aggregate results, no matter how gruesome. This is part of the unleashing process. Posting the results (minus names, of course) lets everyone see how the group views the change. All can see the major issues reinforcing or inhibiting the change. People see whether they are alone in their opposition or support of the idea. Are others frightened or ecstatic? Are others asking the same questions? Survey results give everyone the same picture of reality.

I have gotten good results writing a few provocative questions (five to ten) and sending them out over the company's electronic mail system. E-mail seems to get a much quicker response and a higher rate of return than traditional paper-and-pencil surveys. (If you use electronic mail, make sure that the system allows people to send messages anonymously.) And, as with the formal surveys, use the information as a foundation for further conversation.

### Focus Groups

A focus group is ten to fifteen people who meet one time for about an hour. Its purpose is to gather information: What works? What doesn't?

Safety is key. People need to feel free to talk. Whoever facilitates the conversation needs to listen and paraphrase—and not react. This is no place to get on your podium and sing the virtues of your idea. Your goal is to learn.

I like to go into focus group meetings with a few major questions and then allow what I hear to influence what I ask next. I find that if I am too prepared, with too many questions, I focus more on getting everything covered than on listening and responding to what they are saying.

## PRINCIPLES FOR UNLEASHING

The examples in this chapter honor the five touchstones: Maintain Clear Focus, Embrace Resistance, Respect, Relax, Join with the Resistance. (Obviously, all the approaches listed above begin to Embrace Resistance.) Consider these as you adapt or develop the strategy that will work best for you.

### *Meet Privately at First (Respect, Relax)*

In most of the examples, people worked alone or in small groups before going public with their comments. Find a way to let people think before they speak. Most often they will give you a more thoughtful and considered response. Meeting privately often makes it easier on you as well. You are less likely to feel a need to defend your ideas or reputation.

### *Make It Safe to Speak (Respect, Relax)*

In some organizations, focus groups would not work because trust is so low. In others, people feel free to talk at any time. It is important to pick strategies that fit the organization. If you pick wrong, you'll know. If you hold a Workout and no one comes or few speak, you may have picked the wrong approach for that group at that time.

### *Meet Behind Closed Doors (Relax)*

In the historic 1994 summit between the United States and Russia, Presidents Clinton and Yeltsin decided to hold a part of their talks behind closed doors, without the usual large groups of aides.[4] Meetings like these let people speak much more freely without fear that their comments will be leaked to the press. They can speak off the record. They can disagree in private. And neither player needs to put on a good face for the audience.

Wise employees first introduce new ideas to their bosses privately. It's easier to explore objections openly away from the crowd. In a public forum, some bosses feel the need to appear aloof and authoritative, never admitting weakness or discussing options.

### *People Resist for Good Reasons (Respect)*

From their point of view, people resist your ideas for good reasons. You should keep this in mind as you inquire about their resistance. Don't zing them—just try to learn more about what's on their minds.

### *Don't Penalize the Truth (Respect)*

This links directly to the previous point. Be grateful for honesty; don't kill the messenger.

### *Give Yourself Time to Think (Relax)*
Written comments and survey results give you time to chew and digest before facing those who might oppose or question your idea.

### *Give Them a Target (Maintain Clear Focus)*
The clearer your vision, the stronger the reaction. Ask for what you want. If you're thinking about a restructuring that will close five plants and lay off hundreds, you must tell them.

You have a reason for being excited about this change; others must know what it is. One division director told her staff, "We are facing major challenges over the next few years; I don't believe we are structured to address them adequately. I want us to work together to develop a division that can continually adapt and respond to new challenges." She called in senior management to present their views of the future. She backed up her statement of a need for change with tangible information about the business climate.

A clear statement provides focus and energizes people. Some get excited by the possibility implied in the statement. For others, it raises fear and doubt, and their energy is mobilized as resistance. In both cases you bring them into sync with you on your cycle of change.

When senior management at Deloitte & Touche decided to seek ways to retain and advance more women, reaction within the firm was strong. As you might imagine, some said, "It's about time." Others were skeptical of the leaders' sincerity. Still others believed it would not serve the best interests of clients.

Your statement needs to be clear and impassioned. Clarity lets people know what you are thinking, passion tells them why this is important to you. The stronger the statement, the stronger the reaction.

# 13 DIG BENEATH THE SURFACE

I have not ceased being fearful, but I have ceased to let fear control me. I have accepted fear as a part of life—specifically the fear of change, the fear of the unknown, and I have gone ahead despite the pounding in my heart that says: turn back, turn back, you'll die if you venture too far.
—*Erica Jong*

Often the first response people give you is not the *true* resistance. You need to explore their reactions deeply. For example, your plan to automate procurement procedures won't work because software development will be far too expensive. It could be true that "costs too much" is a fact and that listening to the resistance may save you headaches and dollars. On the other hand, "costs too much" may only be a rational cover hiding a cauldron of boiling resentment. Slowing down, going deeper, lets you get at the real resistance. Perhaps people fear that they lack the skills to work sophisticated programs. Go even deeper: perhaps they fear they are expendable. Deeper yet: they feel worthless. If you are seduced by the "costs too much" argument, you'll search for less expensive ways to develop the new system, thinking you've dealt with the major obstacle, and then wonder why resistance still remains so high.

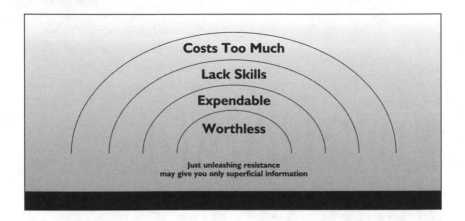

Costs Too Much

Lack Skills

Expendable

Worthless

**Just unleashing resistance
may give you only superficial information**

## LISTENING AND PROBING

To even hope to get people in sync with your plans, ideas, or dreams, you must listen and hear their concerns and fears—both rational and emotional. You must listen to the messages that come from their heads, hearts, and bodies. Let yourself be influenced by what you hear. Then be willing to search for common ground and common purpose. Only by descending into the heart of the resistance can you ever hope to unlock the secret of the question "What's in it for them?"

Once you are willing to engage the deepest fears—theirs as well as yours— you can open a dialogue.

### Take It to the Extreme

When resistance is deep, people are reluctant to tell you what's on their minds. You must keep exploring so you can get deep beneath the surface. You won't accomplish this in a single meeting. If the resistance is deeply entrenched, it could take months to build sufficient trust so that people will tell you the truth.

### Learn Their View of the World

If resistance is deep (Level 2 or beyond), then it is bigger than this particular change. There will undoubtedly be a lot under the surface. You need to learn more about the person or group, not just how they resist you. For example:

- Whom do they serve?
- What pressures do they face from their constituents?
- What money pressures do they face?
- Who judges them? And what do success and failure look like to these judges?
- How do they view you?
- What does a major win look like to them?

- What must they do to save face during this change?
- What do they fear?
- What excites them?

Learning their view of the world can have surprising results. You may well learn that your dreams are similar and begin to see common ground. But, at the very least, the more you learn, the easier it will be for you to plan a change that respects the pressures they face.

## TOOLS FOR EXPLORATION

Whether the resistance is low grade or deeply embedded, you must be willing to explore. All the strategies listed in this chapter rely on one simple and significant skill: listening. From an informal hallway meeting to a Workout, you must be able to hear what people are telling you. The sad news is that most of us are terrible listeners; we formulate our rebuttals instead of attending to what others are saying. Even though you've seen them before, I encourage you to review the listening skills listed below. Think of it this way: Every March some three hundred major-league baseball players report to spring training camps, not to learn new things but to practice the fundamental plays they have been making since they were in grade school. We've been listening since we were born, but how often have we gone to spring training to improve those skills? If highly paid professional athletes can practice the fundamentals, perhaps we should as well.

### *Define Terms*

It is important to use words precisely. We often assume that common terms mean the same to us as they do to others. These untested assumptions can be disastrous. If I believe "business reengineering" means a fundamental reexamination of how our work is organized, and you see it as a less intrusive process, we had better define and agree on terms before we begin a project.

### *Paraphrase*

Using your own words, repeat what you think you heard the other person say. This serves two purposes: it slows you down so that you have to listen before you respond, and it helps you make sure you hear what the other person is saying. When tension is high, your ability to listen diminishes. You hear what you think he meant. Your assumptions hinder your ability to hear. Paraphrasing keeps you listening with open ears.

### *Listen Between the Lines*

As you read this chapter, you can only guess at the tone of voice I would use if I were to read it aloud to you. In places I am sarcastic. For some readers, the words alone will be all the clue they need; for others, it would help to hear the inflection in my voice or see my eyes as I smile. In tense situations, the words alone are usually not the most interesting conversation. So much is being said by people's eyes, tone of voice, body position, pace. And you can only guess at what a furrowed brow might mean, but you can always ask.

### Don't Interrupt

This can be very difficult. The others are attacking your idea, or you personally. It's hard to sit still, but you must. Only in silence can you create the space for others to speak.

Don't interrupt their silence or take the wrong meaning from it. Out of nervousness or haste, you may assume that silence means agreement and try to move on. If you've ever stood in a winter storm, you know that the snow doesn't come in one burst. It may snow heavily for a while, slack off, even quit for a while, then start again. Silence can be like that; people may be thinking, allowing clouds to form. They may be waiting to see what you will do. They may be afraid to say any more. In whatever way you can, show that you truly want to hear all they have to say.

### Listen at Different Levels

When exploring resistance, you must hear the other speakers on many levels— their words, feelings, assumptions, values, wishes, and fears. You must listen for the unspoken. What they are not saying may be more important than their words. If people say they agree to the change, but your instincts tell you that they should be angry—explore. Listen beyond the words to see if you can pick up information from their tone of voice, eye contact, choice of words, how they hold their bodies, or where they choose to sit.

Listen from the heart as well. Resistance cannot be transformed simply by attending to rational concerns. What are the feelings embedded in their statements? Since most resistance stems from fear, you must be willing to listen to those concerns as well. People don't often talk about feelings at work, and when they do they often disguise them. I've heard clients say things like "I took the bullet on that one." Well, I suspect that taking a bullet might hurt. The macho response "took the bullet" is a way of acknowledging feelings indirectly. It's worth exploring. Were we to respond, "Took a bullet?" that might encourage the person to tell us more.

### Feed Back Impressions

Unless you ask, you can never be certain that what you assume is true. Check observations without judgment. "I can't help noticing how quiet it is in here." "If I were in your shoes, I might be wondering if this plan was really a codeword for downsizing."

## GETTING THINGS
## UP ON THE TABLE

Here is a process for beginning to learn about issues that might otherwise remain hidden.

1.    Assemble a group that represents a cross section of the organization—all levels and all interests. The size of the group is less important than making certain that the gathering is a microcosm of the whole.

2.    Have people meet in their own departments (without their bosses) to discuss the items listed in the questionnaire in chapter 8, How Intense Is the Resistance? Groups rate each item and discuss reasons for their responses. Each group posts its responses on flip-chart pads. (Senior managers should form their own groups to respond to these items.)

3.    Working one item at a time, have each group discuss the ranking it gave and the reasons for this score. Although no critiques are allowed, encourage questions to clarify responses.

4.    Ask everyone to help you identify points where scores are similar and places where scores are different.

5.    Ask for reactions throughout the meeting. Be generous in giving your reactions. If you are surprised, say so. If their responses confirm your fantasies, tell them. If you are reassured by their high scores, let them know that as well.

6.    Don't make promises on the spot, but let people know what you plan to do with what you've learned. Make sure you stick to this promise and get back to them with answers or responses.

People want to talk. The simple act of listening to and showing interest in what people have to say gets them talking. If you provide a safe environment and listen with an open heart and mind, people will begin to tell you what's going on.

### Discuss the Undiscussibles

Chris Argyris has written extensively about the undiscussibles in organizations, those things that have a critical impact on effectiveness but that none dare mention (the "dead thing on the table"): the meeting in which staff know that the new marketing plan, the boss's pet project, is ill-conceived; the concern that the CFO doesn't understand the business pressures facing the organization.[1]

| WHAT THEY'RE THINKING | WHAT THEY'RE SAYING |
|---|---|
| | **KATE**<br>So, what do you think about the idea? |
| **JIM**<br>What a boneheaded plan. Where does she get her ideas? | **JIM**<br>Sounds good to me. |
| | **BILL**<br>Absolutely. I'm in . . . |
| | **KATE**<br>Can you spare Jeff and Warren for this? |
| **FRANK**<br>Don't call on me. Don't call on me. Oh, no . . . | **BILL**<br>Sure, whatever you need. |
| | **KATE**<br>So, Frank, how about you? |
| **FRANK**<br>Whew! Made it through that one. | **FRANK**<br>(Hesitates) Ah, sounds fine. I think it'll work if we put dollars behind it. |

When too much is under the table, the probability of success diminishes. Manipulation escalates; this is the only way people believe they can get things done. If a group doesn't believe it can tell you the truth, it will find other ways to get the message to you.

Argyris devised a simple yet effective tool to help groups come to terms with the undiscussibles. It's a good way to unleash and explore resistance—but it's not for the faint of heart. He suggests asking each member of the group to write a script down the right-hand column of the page that replicates how this group usually discusses a particular business issue. This is usually a fairly easy task. Down the left-hand column they write all the things they might be thinking but not saying.

I was working with a group of senior managers who were trying to get a new project off the ground. The meeting went in circles. My interventions did nothing to change the downward spiral of energy. Exasperated, I stopped the meeting and asked, "You've had this conversation before, haven't you?" They nodded. I then described the Argyris script method to them. I asked them to think about the last thirty minutes and write down all the things they had been thinking but not saying. Once they had written these down, I asked whether anyone would be willing to name one of these undiscussible items. Slowly, people responded. Soon they had listed several major undiscussibles. All agreed that these were truly the things that were getting in the way of a decision.

Just getting the issues out in the open helped free the group from their constraints. They had acknowledged that they had a problem and identified many of the things that were creating it. The next step was to begin talking about the recently discussed undiscussibles.

Groups can do the same for each other. Ask one department to identify the things that probably wouldn't be said out loud in the meeting but would have a significant bearing on progress. This allows people to brainstorm issues within the safety of the group, then report out to the full assembly with no attribution to individuals. Once the issues are out in the open, the group can decide which issues to tackle first.

Even though groups should talk about the undiscussibles, just mentioning them takes away much of their power to subvert. Often people breathe easier once it is safe to speak the truth.

Argyris points out that learning how to engage in skillful discussion takes about as much effort as becoming a fair tennis player. In other words, just reading these few paragraphs, or taking that $99, one-day workshop guaranteed to teach you everything you ever wanted to know about communicating, won't be enough.

Digging beneath the surface is hard work. The effort lies not so much in unleashing and exploring; these are fairly straightforward skills. The most important skill is staying calm enough to allow ourselves to use these skills.

# 14 ENGAGE WITH COURAGE

We usually see only the things we are looking for—
so much so that we sometimes see them where they are not.
—*Eric Hoffer*
A Passionate State of Mind

I n *The Inferno,* when Dante passed through the massive stone gates
that read, "Abandon all hope, ye who enter here," he was just beginning his journey.[1] Although it took courage to enter the unknown,
he would need to summon even greater strength to continue
through the Nine Circles of Hell and the Rings of Purgatory in the
belief that this unlikely route would lead him to Paradise.

When we unleash resistance, we too have just begun. Like Dante, we may see
the potential terror that awaits us on the other side of the massive wall, and wish
to turn back. Perhaps we will retreat quickly and congratulate ourselves on at
least getting a glimpse of the other side. But that fleeting, tourist's view of Hell
won't get us to Paradise. We must descend. As someone once said, the only way
up is down.

Many times Dante trembled and wanted to turn back. His guide, Virgil, reminded him of his goal and provided the light to keep him safely on the path. Facing opposition is a lot like that. We may feel as if we have entered a Hell from which there is no return. We look ahead and see only another, even more horrific, circle. We look back and realize that we have left the safety of the woods far behind. And yet, even with the tremendous fear and wonderment of what lies ahead, we may feel an odd sense of exhilaration. Excitement. Stimulation. For some mysterious reason, this journey energizes us.

When resistance is strong, we may enter Hell when someone attacks us or questions our motives. They say, How dare you consider this change? Don't you know what it will do to us? How could you act without heart? How could you be so stupid/venal/insensitive/selfish? That's a lot to take. Often it is enough to make us turn back.

So why do this to ourselves? Dante found that from the safety of the woods there was no direct route to Paradise. Leopards, wolves, and lions blocked all the obvious paths. He had a choice. He could remain in the woods ("How shall I say what wood that was! I never saw so drear, so rank, so arduous a wilderness. Its very memory gives a shape to fear.") or he could attempt to meet his goal by setting off with Virgil. When we unleash resistance, we often get only a hint of the real issues that concern people. If we are tempted to act on that superficial knowledge, we may solve the wrong problem. Remember H. L. Mencken's line: "For every problem there is a simple solution. Neat, easy, and wrong." When the resistance is deep, we cannot see it fully from the safe side of the wall. We must descend.

There is more to Dante's tale than just a harrowing journey. Going beyond the wall that separates the woods from Hell, he leaves behind his ego, his certainty about who he is, and gives in to a faith that he will be transformed by the experience.

## DESPERATELY SEEKING VIRGIL

Exploring resistance is difficult and dangerous. Deep resistance can come as attacks. Comments may make you question your position, what you stand for. The touchstone Maintain Clear Focus becomes perseverance: You must be willing to stay engaged throughout the journey. The touchstone Relax is essential for enduring the heat and keeping a firm footing.

After being stopped by fierce animals on every attempt to reach Paradise, Dante had all but given up on his dream. Then along came Virgil. The poet told Dante that he knew the way and could serve as his guide. During the trip, Virgil provided light to keep Dante on the path, counsel to warn him of dangers, and knowledge of what he was seeing.

Your Virgil can be another person, or it can be a voice within you. Lloyd Richards was my Virgil on that day years ago, and his lightning-rod metaphor continues to help me during tough encounters. As you enter deeply embedded resistance you may value having a Virgil by your side.

In your search for a modern-day Virgil, keep the following key attributes in mind.

### Comes from Outside the Project

Your Virgil should be free from the traps of the content of the project. In other words, he or she should not get hooked by the things that cause you to react to those who resist. If the proposed reorganization is your creation and the slightest criticism causes you to reach for the Prozac, find someone who doesn't have a strong, vested interest in the final shape of the project.

### Attuned to the Surroundings

Virgil should be sensitive to the unspoken, adept at picking up cues from body language or tone of voice. Effective Virgils are as interested in the unspoken as in what's being said.

### Been on the Other Side

Consider a Virgil who has seen the issue from the other side. For example, a union member might be able to help a manager see things she would otherwise have missed.

### Been on a Similar Journey

Virgil should know the way. Perhaps Virgil has taken a similar journey or just has keen instincts about people's reactions to change.

### Is Trustworthy

You must trust, respect, and be willing to listen to Virgil even when you feel trapped in the Seventh Circle of Hell. This person should be able to tell you to shut up and listen, and you should follow the advice, not because you understand why but because you trust that person's wisdom. During the descent, Virgil had to grab Dante and pull him back onto the path out of harm's way.

When Jack Robertson agreed to assist administrator Peter Johnson in beginning a process of public involvement at the beleaguered Bonneville Power Administration, he "asked for his credit card." Robertson was saying, you've got to trust me completely to advise you on these issues. Johnson's willingness to give him his credit card was saying, in effect, that Robertson could be his Virgil for the journey.[2]

## USING VIRGIL

Once you find a Virgil, there are many ways to use him or her. Here are a number of different ways in which you might draw on the wisdom of your modern-day guide.

### *Team Up*

Facing major change alone is a daunting task. Working with a trusted partner can make the load lighter on the journey. If you choose wisely, the two of you can become Virgil for each other; what one misses, the other sees. When one's arrow is about to enter a ring of resistance, the other remains calm. You have an ally with whom you can commiserate, and someone to help you debrief that simple little meeting that has somehow turned into a bloodletting. No doubt Robertson and Johnson filled the Virgil role for each other countless times over the years they worked together.

### *Seek Advice*

Search for people who have successfully implemented ideas similar to yours. Interview them. Listen to their stories. Ask lots of questions. For example:

- How did you build support for the change/idea/new project?
- How did you deal with resistance as it occurred?
- What would you do differently?
- What advice do you have for me?

### *Use a Shadow Consultant*

Often I work alone on projects. Since I assist clients who are either trying to implement a change or are the recipients of someone else's mandate, it is easy for me to get caught up in the resistance swirling around them. If I'm not careful, my own reaction to resistance may cause me to push the client faster than he wants to move on a project. Or I might collude with a client, throwing up my arms and blaming those boneheads in administration for delaying her terrific idea.

Consultants often use shadow consultants to assist them. I do, and they are an important part of my work. They are not part of the project, but consult with me and remain in the shadows for my clients. The client does not pay for or even see them; their usefulness is to me. Since they are free from the minutiae and politics of the project, they provide an unbiased perspective.

My shadow consultants are invaluable. They know me. They know my strengths and my weaknesses. They know what triggers my own resistance. They have learned where I am likely to blunder. We explore instances where I might lose control and react defensively. We explore strategies. We debrief projects. Often we learn as much about ways to handle resistance when we are in the shadow consultant role as when we are asking for guidance. Since we provide this informal service for each other, no money changes hands.

## BECOME YOUR OWN VIRGIL

Virgil need not be someone else. We all have the capacity to draw on the light and strength that Virgil provides. We just need to recognize how we can support ourselves. Two of the touchstones are especially important in finding Virgil: Maintain Clear Focus and Relax.

Virgil never lost sight of the journey's end; neither should you. The clearer you are about the goal, the easier it will be to keep it in mind, even in the depths of the lower circles. In order to endure the pain inherent in exploring resistance, make certain this goal is worth the effort.

Relax, relax, relax. Masters of the Japanese martial art Aikido advise that if your opponent is relaxed, you should relax even more. Just as a willow's branch bends under the weight of snow and springs back once relieved of its burden, you must be bendable and resilient. If you are tense, you will try to hold up the weight of the snow. If it is a light snow, you can keep the branch up, but during a heavy storm your tension will turn to fatigue and cause the limb to break.

How do you relax? There is no one-size-fits-all technique, but here are a few things that might help. Before meeting with the others:

- **SLEEP.** It restores body and mind. This is especially difficult and important, given the pace at which most of us live. Most of us can't do our best work when we are groggy and wondering what time zone our body is in today.

- **EXERCISE.** When I fail to exercise regularly, I feel sluggish and off my game. Exercise also clears my head.

- **DO RELAXATION EXERCISES.** Meditation, yoga, deep breathing, and quiet walks can help calm and clear your head before difficult meetings.[3] Your relaxation need not be mystical or weird—just effective. Just consider what helps you relax.

- **PRACTICE.** Knowing the way before you face others may make the encounter less taxing. Try writing a script of what you might say and what you expect them to say. Of course you will not use the script in a meeting, but it can help you think through how you should handle the situation. Work on reactions to their resistance beforehand. Use the touchstones to develop strategies that let you hear the other person. There is a potential risk in writing a script—

that you will bind yourself to a specific outcome. The reason for the script is to gain comfort, not to predict results.

- **RECALL A HIGHER PURPOSE.** For some, faith provides support. Liz Nappo at Branson Ultrasonics was responsible for implementing a massive employee empowerment process. When I asked where she drew support, she said she was "a pretty spiritual person." She said that she felt we all have a mission and she is living hers. She draws on that and has faith in God that her questions will be answered. Then, as complex and long as the process had been, she spoke of the joy and how easy it was.

During the exchange:

- **POST REMINDERS.** Carry something to remind yourself to use the touchstones. Like the old string around the finger, it helps to have some way to remember to use our skills. During the 1992 presidential campaign, Democratic advisor James Carville posted a sign that read "It's the economy, stupid" to keep himself focused on what was important to voters.

I often draw this simple figure at the top of my note pad. It's my low-budget version of a connect-the-dots picture. It reminds me that I have only a few dots on the page and I'll need many more before I can complete the picture. In other words, I need to 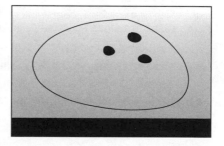 explore the resistance more fully in order to connect the dots. As silly as it might seem, a glimpse of this simple picture can keep me from rushing ahead. It reminds me to pay attention to the person in front of me. It reminds me that my cycle is still at Random Incidents and I will need to gather a lot more information before I can begin to Recognize what's going on.

- **BREATHE.** Oxygen is good; it keeps you alive. Under stress (and dealing with resistance is highly stressful) you tend to stop breathing deeply, depriving your brain of oxygen. Deep breathing can calm you, reminding you to slow down and go deep into the resistance.

- **CHECK THE BODY.** When I get tense, my shoulders tighten and my voice rises. When I recognize these signs, I am often able to relax just by noticing the tension spots. Your tension signs may be different. Pay attention to them.

- **LAUGH.** Self-deprecating humor or jokes that relieve tension can work effectively for some. However, if sarcasm is your favorite form of humor, don't use it.

  Two days after the Republicans took control of Congress in 1994, new Senate Majority Leader Robert Dole was asked if he could work with Newt Gingrich, the new Speaker of the House. This was a major victory for their party; it was a time to build coalitions and repair bridges. Dole commented that he did believe they could work together. And then, as if he couldn't help himself, he said that he had once referred to the Speaker as "the Gingrich who stole Christmas." There was no reason to say this other than that it was funny. It could do nothing to help cement a relationship.

- **IGNORE THE TEMPTATION TO GET EVEN.** Comedians will tell you that dealing with hecklers is difficult. Unless the comedian comes up with a devastating one-liner that silences the jerk, the heckler just keeps on going. Even if the retort works, it alienates at least one member of the audience. Continuing to spar may not only disrupt the comic's timing, it may turn the entire audience against him. They think: If this comedian can attack that guy, he could attack me as well.

  Penn and Teller, the brilliant comedy magicians, began their career performing magic for college audiences. Teller, who remains silent throughout the act, found that hecklers couldn't get him, because he didn't fight back. When they taunted, he said nothing. Looking innocent and bewildered, he would continue with the act. When Penn and Teller refused to join the fight, the resistance soon dissipated.[4] Since most hecklers tend to have a limited repertoire of insults, they quickly run out of things to say. Their power comes from getting the comedians to fight back.

- **GIVE UP EXPECTATIONS.** Serious athletes can become obsessed with time and winning. In *Thinking Body, Dancing Mind,* Jerry Lynch and Chungliang Al Huang discuss the importance of goals and the danger of expectations for athletes:

  > Expectations block your development and limit your horizons. When you have an expectation, you are confident that something will turn out in a particular way. You may be

# THE CONFUSED FRIEND

## AN INTERVIEW WITH TILDEN EDWARDS

*Tilden Edwards, an Episcopal priest, is director of the Shalem Institute for Spiritual Formation in Bethesda, Maryland, and author of many guides to meditative practice. Shalem is dedicated to helping people call forth a deeper spiritual life in themselves and their communities, and Tilden's approach spans religious disciplines, drawing on the contemplative practices of the world's religions. In that resistance seems to be a significant part of most spiritual journeys, I thought his comments might be instructive in secular matters as well.*

**RM:** How does resistance manifest itself in spiritual journeys?

**TE:** Resistance, or unnecessary ego resistance, comes out as a confused friend. It's good as a protective response, but it's gotten exaggerated. It often goes beyond the protection that's really needed. It's like a jack-in-the-box and keeps popping up when you least expect it. It is trying to be a friend of your well-being, but it doesn't know when to stop. For example, when we are angry we tend to focus too intently on the person we are angry with.

**RM:** Are you saying that the anger itself is OK, but the focus on the object of the anger can take it too far?

**TE:** Yes. In Tibetan Buddhist practice, there is an exercise where you give up the object of the anger and focus on the raw energy of the anger. This energy can be very useful, when it's detached from the narrow focus of some object.

**RM:** How do we keep that *good but confused friend* from going too far?

**TE:** Relaxation exercises have a way of showing people the good side of resistance, the shadow side, and what's not necessary. Theologically speaking, everything ultimately is inside God, nothing is outside except in a relative sense. Even resistance then has a divine connection. It is ego energy and the divine at work. But our ego takes it too far when it narrows the resistance to defense of self from an outside object's challenge. It loses the larger potential value of its energy.

**RM:** So relaxation with the aim of loosening attachment of the anger to an object might allow you to transform the anger—create a shift, if you will?

**TE:** Yes, into the raw energy of the anger, which is alive and alert and has great capacity for insight and appropriate action. This free unattached energy can lead us to find a positive invitation in the resistance.

**RM:** How do you and your colleagues keep this confused friend at bay in your work together?

**TE:** Among other things, we use silence. Anyone has a right to call for silence in a meeting and we have seen some incredible transforming things come from these moments. I have seen the whole direction of a meeting shift. I realize you could be strategizing your next moves during the silence, but it is amazing how little I've seen that happen. What it can do is bring people together at a deeper, freer level of awareness.

**RM:** What do you suppose happens in that silence?

**TE:** I think there is a letting go of that confused ego friend, that sense of "I know what's needed here. I know just how to get it, how to manipulate this setup." There is a certain loosening of that sureness and a willingness to enter the unknown, to trust what you don't know. Coming back, there is a childlikeness, where everyone is open to "they don't know what," so to speak. It is a kind of blip that allows a little space for something else to come in (which we would call the Holy Spirit), that otherwise isn't given room to show itself. It catches our egos off guard. We aren't used to shutting up and listening beyond what we and the others present know.

**RM:** Do you use silence in other ways as well?

**TE:** Sometimes we will take turns being silent for a few minutes while others continue with the meeting. There is nothing like being silent when you think your great words are so needed by the group. You discover that there's a lot of good going on without your saying anything, and your silence has a way of helping others stay more open. Silence drops people a little closer to another way of knowing coming through the spiritual heart, or a deeper wisdom.

looking forward to it, as if it were due to happen. Looking forward, however, distracts you from the moment—the task at hand. In the process, you become unfocused and uncentered, pressured and anxious, which interferes with your performance.[5]

When engaging others in resistance, it is best to be open to all possibilities. What they say may be easy to hear, or it may shock you. The stronger your expectations of how it is supposed to go, the more difficult it will be when your expectations are dashed.

The goal of exploration is to fan the flames of resistance. It needs to burn bright. The more you can do to summon its heat, the more chance you will have of getting information that will help you find common ground.

# 15 ACT!

He that leaveth nothing to chance will do few things ill,
but he will do very few things.
—*Lord Halifax*

Throughout this book I have argued that you must get people involved if you want their support. And if their resistance is deep (Level 2 or 3), it is crucial that you use the touchstones to work with their opposition before taking other actions. However, there is one other crucial point: there are times when you must act even without full support. Just as there is a time to explore the resistance and a time to wait for the right opportunity, there is a time to move forward with your idea.

Timing is critical. It isn't easy to know the precise instant when you have built adequate support, but to miss it could be as harmful as acting too soon. In Cleveland, stadium planners realized they had only a few weeks to put a bond issue on the ballot. If they missed this opportunity, they would have to wait another eighteen months. They assessed the support, then moved quickly to get the issue

before the public. Although not everyone in northeastern Ohio was behind the
idea, the planners believed they enjoyed sufficient support to take a chance.

## READ THE SIGNS

How do you know when it's time to act? Weekend boaters seldom set sail in the
middle of a storm, nor do they wait until the air is dead calm. Through experience
on the sea—sometimes harrowing, sometimes maddening in its boredom—
sailors learn to read the wind. Once they are on the water, subtle cues tell them
when to tack and when to open the sails full.

Reading support and resistance is no different. The signs may be small, like
wisps of clouds forming on the horizon. Sometimes the signs may even contradict
one another. Only experience and a willingness to act without complete information allow the sailor and the change agent to move.

Here are a few of the signs.

### Critical Mass

Look at all the groups (and individuals) who have a stake in this change. Do
enough of them support the idea?

A common mistake is to move ahead when just the people in your own circle
agree. That's not enough. Those people think like you do, so of course they like
your idea. The critical mass must come from most, if not all, of the groups.

Some of the signs of critical mass are these:

- **PEOPLE TAKE INITIATIVE ON THE CHANGE WITHOUT DIRECT LEADERSHIP.**
  They are excited enough about the new ideas to offer suggestions and try
  things out on their own. A few years ago I consulted with a department that
  was going through a major restructuring. Although most in the group were
  for the change, Jim and a few colleagues were vocal opponents. Jim seemed
  to hate everything about the proposed change. We tried to involve him in
  decisions; he just complained. But then, one day a couple of months into
  the process, he had a Road to Damascus conversion. He began to see the
  possibilities and the necessity of making the change. As if by magic, he had
  become a champion of the restructuring. That was a turning point in the
  project. It let us know that we could move more easily along the cycle.

- **PEOPLE SPEAK WELL OF THE CHANGE.** Listen for shifts in language from
  negative to positive, from synonyms for impotence to talk of empowerment.
  Listen to the tone of voice when people speak. Are voices somber, as in a
  Bergman film, or are they light? Listen for how people use humor.

Sometimes humor is playful and engaging, at others sarcastic and bitter. If there is too much gallows humor, you may not have the support you need.

Pay attention to informal conversations. People will often give lip service to an idea in meetings. Most of us are wise enough to say the things that will keep us gainfully employed. It is when we are relaxed that our true thoughts and feelings are likely to emerge. That's why the informal conversations are so important to hear. One company president credits his strong constitution for his success at managing. When he tours facilities around the world, he always invites managers out for an evening of dinner and social activities. He stays late, knowing that it will take until the wee hours before people will let down their guard and talk candidly with him.

Remember, be sure not to misread silence as growing support for the idea. Silence may mean support, but it can just as well signal resistance that has gone underground. Silence may indicate that people feel too frightened to speak their minds and hearts.

- **LEADERSHIP FOR THE PROJECT SHIFTS FROM US TO THEM.** Notice who has energy for this work. If you are the only advocate for the change and you find yourself expending a lot of energy trying to keep people motivated, then you probably have not achieved anything near critical mass. Look for signs of a shift such as people creatively approaching the challenges, staff coming to you with ideas, people genuinely excited about moving ahead.

The excitement needs to be shared. When the cycles are joined, it is difficult to tell who originally thought up the idea. People want to move to the next stage.

### Key Players

Every group has a few influential players, men and women whose opinions carry an uncommon weight among their peers. Their support may mean more to your change than the approval of scores of others. Key players must support the change.

When C. Michael Armstrong became chief executive officer at Hughes Aircraft, he had a problem. He was an outsider. He knew little about their business. Before he accepted the job, he spent several days learning all he could about the top seven people in the company. "What I was unsure of was, did Hughes have a top management team that I could go in and work with, and earn their respect, and make that a mutual respect?" He accepted the job and then met with each of the seven. He told each one that he admired his work and wanted him to be part of his team—and gave him a week to decide. According to the *Wall Street Journal*, "His brashness won their respect, as did the detailed knowledge he demonstrated about each of their careers, and in no time he had them agreeing not only to stay on but to carry out his plan for restructuring Hughes and jump-starting revenue growth."[1]

### Cultural Fit
Changes are most successful when they fit into the existing culture. The more closely aligned to the existing culture, the easier the change is likely to be. The more radical the shift, the more difficult the change.

In the early days of the quality movement in the United States, some companies tried to apply processes exactly as they had been used in Japan, grafting a delicate Japanese cherry branch onto an American elm. It simply didn't work. Companies that found ways to adapt quality improvement to their unique cultures fared much better in getting the graft to grow.

### Timing
Some ideas are good, but their timing is wrong. In the 1970s, Harold Sperlich and two other designers came up with the idea for the minivan. Lee Iacocca, president of Ford at that time, loved the idea, but the chairman, Henry Ford II, didn't. It could have been in the way that Sperlich presented it: "I tended to push hard, and that made me unpopular with top management." It could have been Henry Ford's fear that the minimax (as it was called) would become the next Edsel. Or it could have been the high cost of such a project.

Iacocca allowed research to continue, out of the chairman's sight. Sperlich went to Chrysler in 1977, Iacocca in 1978. Still in love with the idea, Iacocca became the champion for this new vehicle. According to *Fortune,* Chrysler "has virtually owned the market" since its introduction in 1983. Estimates are that minivan sales will rise another 40 percent by the end of the decade.[2]

Iacocca's and Sperlich's vision was far ahead of Henry Ford's on this issue. They could see the possibility in the minivan; presumably Ford could see only the reasons to resist. The idea was great; the time and place were wrong. By biding his time, Iacocca was able to create a vehicle that has become a cash cow for Chrysler.

If you are a visionary and can see the future, you must assess whether others can (or are likely to) see it as well. If not, this may not be the time to forge ahead. And as a warning about timing, Henry Ford made Iacocca fire Sperlich.

### Read History
Look at what has worked before. If you work inside an organization, you have seen plenty of changes that demanded the support of others. What sets apart the

changes that worked from those that failed? Does the current change match the profile of those that succeeded? Specifically:

- Does the cycle location of all players match the conditions of the earlier change?

- Are the levels of resistance similar in intensity to the successful change?

- Are your strategies for implementation similar to those of the other change?

- Do you have the same commitment and stamina as those who were champions of the earlier change?

If your answers compare favorably to the successful changes, the time may be right to act. If not, you have four choices:
1. Go ahead at great risk.
2. Give up, realizing that this is not the time.
3. Use the touchstones to develop strategies to work with the resistance.
4. Wait for sufficient wind to set sail.

### Acknowledge the Old
One form of resistance is hanging on to the old ways, sticking with old habits when it's time to move ahead. You need to help people (and yourself) say goodbye to the old and make the transition. In effect, you need to honor any major passing just as you would a death. A funeral is called for.

In organizations we find it hard to allow people to express grief and loss, and yet it is an essential part of letting go of the old. Don't be afraid of hearing about the good old days. It is as important as telling stories about a departed friend.

A health-care system had completed a long-planned merger but people were still hanging onto the old ways of doing things. No one was merging very well. Many were sad over what they were being asked to give up. But there was no way to express these feelings. A colleague and I held a meeting with all the managers. Our approach was quite simple. We asked people to meet in their original organizational groups and discuss what they had gained and what they had lost by the merger. Each group then reported to the whole.

The results were surprising to many in the room. All groups, even those who had received promotions to corporate headquarters as a result of the change, felt deep loss. This sparked the necessary shift. People's use of language changed. In our interviews before the meeting, people talking about the change were using synonyms for powerlessness. By midday of our session, people were beginning to use synonyms for empowerment. They were talking about what they could do to make the merger work.

The change occurred because people were being allowed to speak from their hearts. Too often our changes are technically perfect—the boxes are neatly arranged, columns add up, procedures are in place—but we fail to acknowledge the human aspect.[3]

### Know When to End

Sometimes your idea is a lost cause. You should bury it and move on. It is important to distinguish between perseverance and bullheaded tenacity. There is an old cartoon in which two soldiers arise from their foxhole to look out over a world completely destroyed, no one left alive. One soldier turns to the other and says, "I think we won."

### ACT!

An old proverb reads, "When you stand, stand. When you sit, sit. But most of all, don't wobble." Once you decide, act!

The planners in Cleveland moved quickly and strongly to get on the ballot. One exciting aspect of large-systems change models like Future Search and Real Time Strategic Change is that they can propel movement. When these events work successfully, people are ready to join and act with you.

In Aikido, a skilled practitioner waits attentively for the attacker to move. If he were to wait too long, the attacker could harm him. He waits until the perfect moment, then moves with energy. There is nothing languid or weak in the master's movements; he just waits until that perfect moment to respond.

### Find a Marco Polo

Seizing the moment need not be a Cecil B. DeMille production. Actions can be small but decisive. In 1980, Ford decided to improve the quality of its manufacturing process. Instead of making a grand executive pronouncement and trumpeting the change throughout the company, they started small. They searched for the Marco Polos of Ford—plant managers and union stewards willing to sign onto an adventurous journey without much of a map. When they found these Marco Polos, they invited them to pilot test quality improvement processes.

For three years, these test sites worked on quality improvement. Word got out—something different was going on at these locations. Interest built within the company. Once Ford had worked out the bugs and given others an opportunity to witness the test, they introduced quality improvement to the entire company.[4]

Test runs give people models. They can see whether it plays in Peoria. They can watch others implement the change. Getting a chance to see the change in action often dissipates concerns. However, it is important that the test site not be held up as something special or better than the rest. If that occurs, the rest of the organization is likely to dismiss the test.

### *Support Change Agents*

You will probably need to count on others to help carry out the change. If the risks are too high and failures too frequent, you could find resistance developing among the people you were counting on. Being on the leading edge of a change can be risky and dangerous and these people need support. Jack Robertson of the Bonneville Power Administration suggests building a cocoon around that first round of change agents. Here's what a cocoon looks like:

- **SHORT-TERM SUCCESSES.** The change agents need to feel an early success. Establish incremental plans that allow people to see small wins.

- **ARCHITECTURE FOR THE CHANGE.** Robertson suggests thinking of support in concentric circles. The first circle is the group that will lead the change. The second circle holds those groups and crucial individuals who must initially support the change, and so forth. An architecture is a plan for change that enables the change agents to know where they are going.

- **PROTECTION FROM FAILURE.** Robertson believes that there needs to be a high degree of probability that these people will succeed.

- **EMOTIONAL COMMITMENT.** Change agents will need all the support you can give them. They must know that you are not just behind them, but working with them to ensure that the change is successful. When there is a win, share it. And when there is a setback, share that as well.

### *Move Without Support*

When Leonard Bernstein became conductor of the Vienna Philharmonic, he reintroduced the symphonies of Gustav Mahler. The orchestra hated Mahler; they felt his music was overblown and pompous. Bernstein was undeterred. He scheduled the symphonies into programs.[5] Although Bernstein certainly had the power to program whatever he wished, it was a risky move. Orchestras notoriously show their disdain for conductors they don't respect by engaging in malicious compliance. All the notes are correct—so no one can be reprimanded—but they play without spirit. It makes for a very boring evening.

Although Bernstein did not enjoy support for the decision to play Mahler, he was highly respected by the members of the orchestra. He had been a frequent guest conductor. They had seen him in action and knew his formidable skills. He was a world-class musician. So, for Leonard Bernstein, they played Mahler beautifully. Eventually, it seems, most of the orchestra grew to enjoy playing the music of their hometown boy.

Robert Frey also moved without much support as he tried to implement profit sharing at Cinmade. Like Bernstein, he was respected, and was certain of the rightness of his decision.

Moving without support is always tricky, and it seldom works if the resistance is deep. You may be able to push through Level 1 resistance if you enjoy the credibility of a Bernstein or Frey, but you run a serious risk of failure if the resistance is stronger.

If you must move, consider the following:

- What impact will this change have on the people who must support it? Will it benefit or harm them? (If the change will be harmful, then you risk hurting others and losing your credibility.) No one was hurt—no one would lose a job or status—by playing the symphonies of Mahler.

- Is there a compelling reason for moving ahead without listening to their concerns and getting others involved? Are you sure? What does your Virgil advise?

- Are you 100 percent certain that this change will benefit those people?

- Are you the Leonard Bernstein of your organization? Do people respect your knowledge, judgment, and world-class abilities?

- Do you so believe in this change that you are willing to take tremendous heat for a very long time? Are you willing to descend with only Virgil at your side, not seeing light for an indefinite amount of time?

If your candid response to those questions supports the decision to move ahead, good luck. While implementing the change, you can and should use the touchstones to listen to concerns, respond to criticisms, and be influenced by the wisdom of others.

### Go for Understanding

If after a sincere effort there is no agreement, then you need at least to make sure people understand where you are going. Senior staff in one organization were attempting to explain to the CEO that they didn't agree with the course he was about to take.

They debated the issue for a while. People did listen to each other, but it was clear that they could not come to an agreement. The CEO thanked them for their suggestions, said that he was not convinced by their arguments, and wanted to proceed. What was important was that they all were clear about the course they were going to take.

Obviously, this approach can be misused. If he gave only lip service to their arguments, he could not count on their long-term support. However, if he truly listened and tried to find ways to incorporate their suggestions, he would have a much better chance of enjoying their commitment to the idea.

### *Offer Yourself As a Sacrifice*

Sometimes the only way to move ahead is to remove yourself from the situation. When Stephen Wolf tried to save United Airlines by championing employee ownership, union opposition was strong; a "chasm of suspicion" separated management and labor. Though Wolf didn't create the problem, neither did his management style do much to solve it. Unrest continued to mount. Mechanics carried a coffin with his name on it across the tarmac in San Francisco.

A spokesperson for the Pilots' Union said, "The principal reason I feel Mr. Wolf should not be CEO is that, in talking to him, I just don't think his mind set fits into employee ownership." Wolf made the decision to leave his post in order to remove a major obstacle to the change.[6]

## KEEP MOVING

Once you take action, you may expect resistance to fade away. If you have engaged others in candid dialogue, allowed yourself to be influenced by others, showed patience that would rival Job, you want the hard stuff to be over. It isn't.

The cycle keeps moving. As it moves, fresh resistance develops. It may be conflict over strategies or time lines. Something outside your control changes the relationship between you and a key group of would-be supporters. Funding changes, throwing agreements into disarray.

There will always be people who are late in accepting the change. They deserve the same respect and attention as those who were astute enough to accept your idea the day you presented it. Even though some are late in arriving, they will need your support and help in implementing the change.

Resistance never ends. It is the lifeblood of change. It is the desperately needed traction that keeps us from careening off the road during an ice storm. Once we accept the fact that resistance exists and will never go away, the easier it will be to embrace it and use its energy to build support for change.

As we move, we will err. We are human, after all. Even those who handle resistance elegantly have bad days. What distinguishes the best is not that they use the

# TIMING
## AN INTERVIEW WITH ROSE HARVEY

*Rose Harvey is regional vice president in the New York office of the Trust for Public Land. TPL's mission is to save land for people, with a strong emphasis on community park land near where people live, play, and work. In many instances TPL protects land by securing it, then transferring it to public agencies for use as park land. Even when landowners want to sell, there can still be plenty of resistance to the deal. Owners may believe their land is worth more than they are being offered or object to the terms of the sale. I was particularly interested in Harvey's thoughts on the importance of timing in coming to agreement.*

**RM:** How important is timing?

**RH:** Timing is everything. If you don't have it, you've got to leave. We've left many deals and come back in a year just to let things play out.

**RM:** What might play out?

**RH:** The landowner may have an inflated expectation of the land's value. If that's the case and they really believe it, you don't have a prayer. It doesn't matter what you do. You've got to wait until they realize their price is too

high. Unless they need the money badly or there is some other leverage point, you've got to be willing to walk away and let circumstances (i.e., the market, regulation, environmental advocacy) educate them and create these leverage points.

**RM:** I'd think that would be extremely difficult to do. After all the time you have invested in a land deal, how do you just walk away?

**RH:** It's much easier to walk away if you know you will have a second chance. But if you're dealing with someone who has the permits in place and can begin development the minute your negotiations fall through, and you have exhausted all remedies, you must realize that you are wasting time. You've got to remember that you could be using that time to save another piece of land. There are alternatives. There may be three separate properties that could provide exquisite park land opportunities for a community. That makes it easier to walk away.

You've got to believe in yourself and in your ability to read the situation and to do the best possible job to close the deal. If not, you may hit your head against the wall forever. But walking away is the hardest thing any of our project managers must do. That's the first lesson they have to learn and it's the hardest one as well. We usually partner just because it helps to have another person looking at the situation. Also, we provide a fair amount of oversight from people who have been in the trenches. They can help the project manager really evaluate the situation to see if it's worthwhile to keep on going. We are constantly calling our project managers and telling them to cool out.

**RM:** But if you walk away, how do you meet your goals?

**RH:** In most instances the walk away is temporary until timing improves or circumstances change. In those instances where you might lose the property if you walk away, then you've got to be sure you've explored all alternatives. The issue might be changing your goals or strategies: it might be a partial acquisition, a land swap, or allowing the landowner a life estate, to ensure that every possible alternative has been explored. If there are no alternatives, then we have no options. If it's not a willing seller, or we're never going to be able to raise the money they want, then we're going to be most effective walking away early on and investing our time in projects that will work. No one's mission is going to be accomplished by banging their head against a wall or working endless hours on a project that's never going to work.

In the '90s we need to work in partnership with landowners and have more realistic goals. When we go out to buy a property and are unable to do so, we need to draw back and think about revising our goals and measure those new goals against our original ones to make sure we aren't sacrificing our original intent or mission. In many cases the same end goal can be achieved through a different means.

touchstones 100 percent of the time, but that they can see when they have moved off course and know how to get back on track.

## PLAN FOR THE FUTURE

It is not too early to begin thinking about the next change, and the one after that. The extent to which we build trust and support today will serve us well in changes to come. It will build a base that increases the likelihood that resistance to the next change will be minimal. People might resist our ideas, but they will be less likely to question our motives or look back to changes we botched in the past.

We are just beginning to understand how to consistently build support for change within organizations. We have a lot to learn. Perhaps your experiments at building cooperation will help us all see other possibilities. Given the pace of change, there will certainly be no shortage of opportunities to practice.

Change and resistance do not have to be mortal enemies. As I write this, many are making the unconventional a way of life. The more we attempt these experiments in embracing resistance, the more we will shine Virgil's light and illuminate the path for others. I wish you well.

# NOTES,
# RESOURCES,
# AND TOOLS

## NOTES

### *Chapter 1*

1. Hal Lancaster, "Reengineering Authors Reconsider Reengineering," interview with Michael Hammer and James Champy, *Wall Street Journal,* January 17, 1995.
2. Anne B. Fisher, "How to Make a Merger Work," *Fortune,* January 24, 1994, 66. McKinsey's research covered a ten-year period. The American Management Association studied fifty-four large mergers in the late '80s and found that approximately one-half "led straight downhill in productivity, profits, or both."
3. William Schiemann, "Why Change Fails," *Across the Board,* April 1992.

4. Linda Moran, Jerry Hogeveen, Jan Latham, and Darlene Russ-Eft, *Winning Competitive Advantage: A Blended Strategy Works Best* (San Jose, Calif.: Zenger-Miller, 1994). Just over one-third of respondents to a survey on implementation of quality improvement reported internal resistance to their efforts. From that group only 43 percent believed that they were making satisfactory progress. Seventy-five percent of the resistance came from middle managers, 63 percent from front-line managers and supervisors.

5. Jim Johnson, "Chaos: The Dollar Drain of IT Project Failures," *Application Development Trends,* January 1995, 41. Research indicated that a staggering 31.1 percent of all projects will get canceled before they ever get completed. Further results indicate 52.7 percent of projects will overrun their initial cost estimates by 189 percent.

6. Resistance is a subject filled with paradox. Giving strength to resistance by trying to destroy it is the first of many such paradoxes that appear in this book.

## Chapter 2

1. *The New Grolier Multimedia Encyclopedia,* Release 6, 1993.
2. ISO 9000 is a set of quality standards created by the International Standards Organization in an effort to ensure interchangeability of parts.
3. David Kenney, "Quality Standards That Can Destroy Quality," *Wall Street Journal,* November 11, 1993.
4. Unless the stories about organizations come from the business press or personal interviews, I disguise the names and types of business.
5. Mark Stahlman, "Creative Destruction at IBM," *Wall Street Journal,* January 6, 1993. Stahlman suggests that IBM did not realize how big the PC market would be. Its initial forecast was for a total of 200,000 PCs to be sold. Today, that many are sold every week.

## Chapter 3

1. Theodor Seuss Geisel ("Dr. Seuss"), *Green Eggs and Ham* (New York: Beginner Books, 1960).
2. Series of articles that ran in the *Washington Post* and *Washington Business Journal* in 1992 and 1993. I find it interesting that the owner, Jack Kent Cooke, has since tried to move his team to Laurel, Maryland, and two other suburban locations, so far, without success.
3. Interview with Irvin Lipp, formerly Manager, Environmental Issues, External Affairs, Du Pont, November 1994.

4. Default positions are the automatic settings on software. For example, unless I do something to override the embedded commands in my word-processing program, it will automatically give me certain margins and line spacing.
5. David Halberstam, *The Best and the Brightest* (New York: Random House, 1972), 201.
6. William Glaberson, "Week in Review," *New York Times*, October 9, 1994.
7. *Columbia Encyclopedia*, 5th ed., 1993.
8. Robert B. Cialdini, *Influence* (New York: Quill, 1984), 254–55. Before this fiasco, *Patton*, the highest-priced rental, went for $1.3 million less than *The Poseidon Adventure* for a single showing on network television.
9. Avinash Dixit and Barry Nalebuff, *Thinking Strategically* (New York: W. W. Norton, 1991). This is a very clear explanation of game theory (without the math) replete with examples from many different types of situations.
10. I recommend David Noer's *Healing the Wounds: Overcoming the Trauma of Layoffs and Revitalizing Downsized Organizations* (San Francisco: Jossey Bass, 1993). Noer describes the pain that downsizing inflicts on the survivors and suggests strategies for rebuilding trust in the organization.

### Chapter 4

1. Interviews in 1993 with people involved with the domed stadium and the Gateway projects. Also a series of articles in the *Cleveland Plain Dealer* from 1983–1994.
2. Lipp interview.
3. Philip Roth, "Juice or Gravy? How I Met My Fate in a Cafeteria," *New York Times Book Review*, September 18, 1994.
4. Thanks to Marc Young for providing the fun house metaphor.
5. Michael Goodman, "Systems Thinking as Language," *The Systems Thinker*™ 2, no. 3 (April 1991). Reprinted by permission of Pegasus Communications, Inc. (Cambridge, Mass.).
6. Barbara Tuchman, *The March of Folly* (New York: Ballantine Books, 1990), 23.
7. David Bohm, *On Dialogue* (Ojai, Calif.: David Bohm Seminars; distributed by Pegasus Communications, Cambridge, Mass., 1990).
8. Everett M. Rogers, *Diffusion of Innovations*, 3rd ed. (New York: Free Press, 1983), 32. Copyright © 1962, 1971, 1983 by The Free Press, an imprint of Simon and Schuster, Inc. Reprinted with permission of the publisher. See the Resources section for more about this fine book.

## Chapter 5

1. Text excerpt from *Duck Soup* used by permission. Copyright © by Universal City Studios, Inc. Courtesy of MCA Publishing Rights, a Division of MCA, Inc. All rights reserved.
2. Some at the Gestalt Institute of Cleveland talk about seeing with soft eyes. By this they mean that we need to keep our focus a bit diffuse so that we can see things on different levels and not get locked into a single view of a situation. I believe this is similar to, if not the same as, having the ability to look near and far at the flick of a focal point.
3. Robert Frey and staff, presentation at Association for Quality and Participation conference, April 1994. See the Resources section for *Harvard Business Review* article by Frey.
4. Tony Snow, commentary on "News Roundup," the *Diane Rehm Show,* WAMU Radio, Washington, D.C., April 14, 1995.
5. Robert Wright, *The Moral Animal: The New Science of Evolutionary Psychology* (New York: Pantheon, 1994), 280.
6. Ed Nevis, comments made at the Gestalt Institute of Cleveland, 1992.
7. Thomas F. Crum, *The Magic of Conflict* (New York: Simon and Schuster, 1987).
8. William Reed, *Ki: A Practical Guide for Westerners* (New York: Japan Publications, 1986), 109.
9. Ibid., 175.
10. Crum, *Magic,* 148.
11. *Morning Edition,* National Public Radio, February 2, 1994. Broadcast included the quotation from Mark Reisner, *Cadillac Desert* (New York: Viking, 1986).
12. Thanks to Max Stark for suggesting that there might be a "shadow side" to the touchstones, then exploring the possibility with me.

## Chapter 6

1. The award was given by Catalyst, a national research and advisory organization that works with corporations and professionals to effect change for women. My thanks to Deloitte & Touche for allowing me to use this story. I first learned of this initiative when Harbridge House invited me to facilitate a number of sessions. In addition, I interviewed Ellen Gabriel, head of the Women's Initiative Task Force; Jim Wall, director of human resources; and Tom Murphy, assistant to the CEO and managing partner.
2. The firm they chose was Harbridge House (Chicago), a leader in dealing with workplace diversity issues.

3. Jane Wagner, *Signs of Intelligent Life in the Universe,* 1986. This is the one woman play in which Lily Tomlin performed on Broadway and around the country.

## Chapter 8

1. Felix Grant, quoted in Ken Ringle, "Felix Grant, for the Love of Jazz," *Washington Post,* November 12, 1989, G1.
2. Rogers, *Diffusion of Innovations,* 15–16. Copyright © 1962, 1971, 1983 by The Free Press, an imprint of Simon and Schuster, Inc. Used by permission of the publisher.
3. Peter Block, *The Empowered Manager* (San Francisco: Jossey-Bass, 1988).
4. Luther Cochrane, "Not Just Another Quality Snow Job," *Wall Street Journal,* May 24, 1993.
5. Daryl Connor, *Managing at the Speed of Change* (New York: Villard, 1993). Connor writes well about the importance of resilience and how we are running out of it due to the pace of change.
6. Alex Gibney, "Paradise Tossed," *Washington Monthly,* June 1986, 24–35. The chairman, by the way, was Frank Borman.
7. Interview with Mary Jacksteit and Adrienne Kaufmann, OSB, co-directors of the Common Ground Network for Life and Choice, April 24, 1995. Also interview by Fred Fisk on the *Fred Fisk Show,* February 19, 1994, WAMU Radio, Washington, D.C.
8. Perhaps there is a Level 4, a degree of intensity so deep that it is impossible to build common ground. Certainly there are those rare instances in which we must not attempt to build common ground because the situation is unethical or illegal. But are there hopeless situations? I'm not sure.
9. Thanks to Matt Kayhoe for adding to and helping to clarify my thinking on the relative degrees of intensity, and for helping me see the interplay among the levels.
10. One caveat: If you don't plan to get people involved (in other words, if you don't accept the basic premise of this book), then don't invite staff to complete the questionnaire. Just asking these questions indicates a desire on your part to hear the answers and respond. To ask for information you will never use breeds well-deserved cynicism.

## Chapter 9

1. I first heard Peter Block ask the question "What's your contribution to the problem?" years ago. It still serves as a good all-purpose question to ask myself and my clients. It invariably reveals invaluable data.

2. David Cooperrider and Suresh Srivastva have developed a process for organizational change called appreciative inquiry. It is based on the belief that all organisms are heliotropic, that is, they move toward the sun or life-giving forces. They suggest that, rather than focusing on what's wrong, it is better to find those life-giving forces already present within the organization. These practices can become the foundation for renewal. See *Appreciative Management and Leadership* (San Francisco: Jossey-Bass, 1990) for more details.

### Chapter 10

1. Thanks to Kathie Dannemiller for her help in reminding me of the importance of the shift. (And for using the term "shift" to describe it. It's so clear and simple.)
2. Skunk works was an informal group of engineers who organized because they couldn't bear to see the name "Mustang" sold to a foreign manufacturer. They had to convince leadership that the company could produce the car in half the time, at half the cost, and still meet Ford's stringent quality standards. The skunk works studied the situation and succeeded in convincing management that it was possible. It was their story that all 2,400 employees heard that morning.
3. Interview with Kathie Dannemiller, April 2, 1995.
4. Richard Beckhard, "Strategies for Large System Change," in *Organization Development Theory, Practice, and Research,* rev. ed., eds. W. L. French, C. H. Bell, Jr., and R. A. Zawacki (Plano, Tex.: Business Publications, 1983). Beckhard credits David Gleicher with this model, although it is generally attributed to Beckhard.
5. The quote is a paraphrase, since I heard it recounted by the administrator months after the event occurred.
6. Presentation at the Association for Quality and Participation national conference, April 1989.

### Chapter 11

1. Jack R. Gibb, "Defensive Communication," *Journal of Communication* 2, no. 3 (1961), 141–148.
2. In *Healing the Wounds,* David Noer discusses the impact of downsizing on people and organizations. I find it surprising that downsizing is so popular, given its poor record of success. If it actually increased anything (quality, return on investment, etc.), I could see why people would be tempted to con-

sider it, but the reports in the business press indicate that few of these blood-lettings show any tangible benefit.

3. Interview with Marshall Orr, a consultant in Richmond, Virginia, who has used this approach extensively, January 1995.

4. Robert Jacobs, *Real Time Strategic Change* (San Franscisco: Berrett-Koehler, 1994). Jacobs describes the process he uses to work with groups of a few hundred. It is a highly structured model, as it would have to be to work with a group that large, and it is effective.

5. See the Resources section for more on Future Search.

6. Jacksteit and Kaufmann interview. See the Resources section to learn more about this fine organization and its approach.

7. Interviews with James DeGraffenreidt and Jan Chapman, April 1995.

## *Chapter 12*

1. Peter Block has often said that if you really want to know what's going on in an organization, hang around the restrooms during breaks in meetings. In his wonderfully dry manner, he goes on to say that he carries extra shoes so he can sit in a stall incognito. In fairness to all, wouldn't it be wise to make all restrooms unisex?

2. I believe it was Will Schutz who first used this image to describe issues that are too hot to notice or discuss.

3. Noel Tichy and Sherman Stratford, *Control Your Destiny or Someone Else Will* (New York: Doubleday, 1993), 245–246. Used by permission of the publisher.

4. Ann Devroy, "U.S., Russia Sign Variety of Pacts as Talks Focus on Economics," *Washington Post,* September 29, 1994, A25.

## *Chapter 13*

1. Chris Argyris, *Overcoming Organizational Defenses* (Boston: Allyn and Bacon, 1990). Argyris has written extensively about "organizational defensive routines." You might search *Harvard Business Review* as well as his other books for more information.

## *Chapter 14*

1. Dante Alighieri, *The Inferno,* trans. John Ciardi (New York: Mentor, 1954). Copyright 1954 by John Ciardi.

2. Interviews with Peter Johnson, former administrator of the Bonneville Power Administration, and Jack Robertson, his chief of staff. See the Resources section for a description of the *Harvard Business Review* article and the Center for Excellence in Government publication on BPA's public involvement process.
3. See the Resources section for suggestions. In particular, consider *Peace Is Every Step* by Thich Nhat Hanh (New York: Bantam, 1991).
4. Penn and Teller, *Inside the Comedy Mind,* interview by Alan King on the Comedy Central Network, 1994.
5. Chunglaing Al Huang and Jerry Lynch, *Thinking Body, Dancing Mind* (New York: Bantam, 1992).

## Chapter 15

1. Jeff Cole, "Gentle Persuasion: New CEO at Hughes Studied Its Managers, Got Them on His Side," *Wall Street Journal,* March 30, 1994.
2. Alex Taylor III, "Iacocca's Minivan," *Fortune,* May 30, 1994.
3. I highly recommend William Bridges's book on transitions, *Managing Organizational Transitions* (Reading, Mass.: Addison-Wesley, 1991). Bridges writes clearly about this critical stage of the change process.
4. Interview in 1991 with Nancy Badore, head of Ford's executive development process, for my first book, *Caught in the Middle* (Portland, Ore.: Productivity Press, 1992). Also, Badore's speech at the 1990 Organization Development Network conference.
5. "The Gift of Music," television special on Leonard Bernstein, Amberson Productions and WNET, 1993.
6. Richard M. Weintraub, "Stephen Wolf's Bittersweet Farewell," *Washington Post,* February 20, 1994.

Adizes, Ichak. *Corporate Lifecycles: How and Why Corporations Grow and Die and What to Do About It.* Englewood Cliffs, N.J.: Prentice Hall, 1988. Adizes looks at stages of human development as an analogy for organizational change. He suggests that natural resistance occurs when an organization tries to move from one stage to the next, much like a person's growing pains. I find his model intriguing and helpful.

Aikido. This is a fairly recent Japanese martial art whose aim in fighting is to achieve harmony. In its purest form there would be no fights, since there are no attacking moves. One form of the art, Ki Aikido, tends to emphasize the control and use of energy along with the "fighting" moves. Many communities offer instruction.

Alighieri, Dante. *The Inferno.* Verse translation by John Ciardi. New York: Mentor, 1954. I truly enjoy reading this translation. This portion of *The Divine Comedy* is an excellent metaphor for the struggle between our desire to change and the inevitable resistance we create for ourselves.

Argyris, Chris. *Overcoming Organizational Defenses: Facilitating Organizational Learning.* Boston: Allyn and Bacon, 1990. Argyris has written extensively about ways to get undiscussibles out in the open. This book is but one of many treatments on the subject. Also see his *Harvard Business Review* articles on the subject.

Block, Peter. *Flawless Consulting: A Guide to Getting Your Expertise Used.* San Diego: Pfeiffer and Company, 1981. The entire book is a helpful manual, but the chapters on resistance offer sound suggestions for ways in which consultants can work with those who resist.

Bohm, David. *On Dialogue.* Ojai, Calif.: David Bohm Seminars; distributed by Pegasus Communications, Inc. (Cambridge, Mass.), 1990. Bohm is generally credited with arguing for the importance of dialogue. This small book is the text of a presentation he gave on dialogue.

Bridges, William. *Managing Organizational Transitions: Making the Most of Change.* Reading, Mass.: Addison-Wesley, 1991. Bridges argues that the reason we are so poor at beginning things is that we don't know how to end what came before. I agree. This fine book offers the reader practical tools to approach the transition from old to new.

Conner, Daryl. *Managing at the Speed of Change: How Resilient Managers Succeed and Prosper Where Others Fail.* New York: Villard, 1993. Conner has good things to say about the nature of change. His section on how change wears down our resilience is especially interesting.

Crum, Thomas. *The Magic of Conflict: Turning a Life of Work into a Work of Art.* New York: Simon and Schuster, Touchstone, 1987. This is a practical application of Aikido to our lives. Well written.

Fisher, Roger, and William Ury. *Getting to Yes: Negotiating Agreement Without Giving In.* New York: Penguin, 1983. This perennial bestseller is a down-to-earth guide on ways to use principled negotiation to create agreements in which all sides can win. The advice in this book can extend to any situation in which you want to gain influence with others.

Frey, Robert. "Empowerment or Else," *Harvard Business Review* 71, no. 5 (September/October 1993). This is the first-person account of how Frey turned Cinmade into an organization that is productive and cares about people.

Gestalt psychology. Many cities have gestalt institutes. This branch of psychology has had a profound influence on my thinking about resistance. If you can get past jargon such as retroflection and introjection, gestalt concepts are sound and practical. For those with a specific interest in how gestalt theory applies to organizations, there is no better place to study than the Gestalt Institute of Cleveland.

Hanh, Thich Nhat. *Peace Is Every Step: The Path of Mindfulness in Everyday Life.* New York: Bantam, 1991. This is a fine book, filled with simple and practical ways to pay attention to what's in front of you. Very helpful when attempting to stay open to resistance.

*I Ching.* This ancient book is a basic foundation for two of the world's great religions, Taoism and Confucianism. The *I Ching* suggests that change is constant. Although some use the book as an oracle, I find it helpful as a way of seeing the current state and recognizing the subtle and profound forces that push change to the next phase. This book is esoteric and difficult to comprehend.

There are many translations. I encourage you to browse in a good library or a large bookstore to find the translation that seems clearest to you.

Jacksteit, Mary, and Adrienne Kaufmann. *Finding Common Ground in the Abortion Conflict: A Manual.* Washington, D.C.: The Common Ground Network for Life and Choice, 1995. This manual for facilitating structured dialogue is quite good (and its application is broader than a single topic), and at the time of publication, the cost was only ten dollars. That is an unbelievable bargain. The address is 1601 Connecticut Avenue, N.W., Washington, D.C. 20009.

Jacobs, Robert. *Real Time Strategic Change: How to Involve an Entire Organization in Fast and Far-Reaching Change.* San Francisco: Berrett-Koehler, 1994. This is a thorough and compelling description of the change process mentioned in chapter 10, Create the Shift. If you want even more detail, try *Real Time Strategic Change: A Consultant's Guide to Large-Scale Meetings* (Ann Arbor: Dannemiller-Tyson, 1994). This is a bible for people who want to use this approach. Expensive, but worth every dollar.

Johnson, Peter. "How I Turned a Critical Public into Useful Consultants," *Harvard Business Review* 71, no. 1 (January/February 1993). This is a first-person account of the ways in which the Bonneville Power Administration increased public involvement. It is a detailed account of how to build support for change. Also, you might be interested in reading *Public Involvement: The Bonneville Power Story* (Washington, D.C.: The Council for Excellence in Government, 1995).

Karp, Hank. *Personal Power: An Unorthodox Guide to Success.* New York: AMACOM, 1985. Although the book covers much more than resistance, the chapters on the subject are straightforward and practical.

Lao-tzu. *Tao Te Ching.* This ancient book of wisdom suggests that it is best to act in accordance with the forces at hand. There are many fine translations. I particularly like Steven Mitchell's (New York: Harper and Row, 1988) and the version by Gia-fu Feng and Jane English (New York: Knopf, 1972).

Nevis, Edwin. *Organizational Consulting: A Gestalt Approach.* New York: Gestalt Institute of Cleveland Press, 1987. Chapter 8 presents a clear discussion of the use of resistance in organizational consulting. I recommend this book for consultants who want to learn how to apply gestalt theory in their client engagements.

Noer, David. *Healing the Wounds: Overcoming the Trauma of Layoffs and Revitalizing Downsized Organizations.* San Francisco: Jossey-Bass, 1993. Noer discusses the psychic and economic costs to individuals and organizations from downsizing. He offers ways to begin healing those wounds. Better to find alternatives to downsizing, but if the deed is already done, I recommend this book.

Owen, Harrison. *Open Space Technology: A User's Guide.* Potomac, Md.: Abbott Publishing, 1993. Owen has developed a radical approach to change. With minimal structure and facilitator interference, large groups of people can create an agenda and complete a significant amount of work in a short time. Since everyone can be involved to whatever level he or she chooses, this tends to reduce resistance and build support for the process.

Price Waterhouse. *Better Change: Best Practices for Transforming Your Organization.* New York: Irwin, 1995. A short and practical guide to organizational change. There is a lot packed into these pages.

Rogers, Everett. *Diffusion of Innovations,* 4th ed. New York: Free Press, 1995. This is a wonderful book, filled with research on ways in which cultures and groups have either built support for innovations or killed them. Although the focus is primarily on technological change, the principles apply broadly.

Ryan, Kathleen, and Daniel Oestreich. *Driving Fear Out of the Workplace: How to Overcome the Invisible Barriers to Quality, Productivity, and Innovation.* San Francisco: Jossey-Bass, 1991. These authors write convincingly about the power of fear to destroy productivity. In my words, they are writing about one important aspect of Levels 2 and 3 resistance.

Spencer, Laura. *Winning Through Participation: Meeting the Challenge of Corporate Change with the Technology of Participation.* Dubuque, Iowa: Kendall/Hunt Publishing, 1989. This is a practical little book, filled with many ways to get people involved in planning and problem solving. The approach has been used around the world, in villages and corporations. The methods are simple and can be used by anyone.

T'ai Chi Chuan. This is an old Chinese martial art that is graceful and calming. It is based on the principle that energy moves from one pole to the other and that the way to be successful is to act in harmony with that energy. The main form of sparring, called "push hands," is an exercise in simplicity and humility that shows the absolute necessity of staying relaxed when facing resistance. Courses are offered in many cities. Look around.

Ury, William. *Getting Past No: Negotiating with Difficult People.* New York: Bantam, 1991. A worthy follow up to Fisher and Ury's *Getting to Yes.* This is a book of strategies that offers what the title suggests.

U.S. Department of Labor. *Guide to Responsible Restructuring.* Washington, D.C.: GPO, 1995. A thirty-five page booklet that describes research on the cost of downsizing (there seem to be few benefits) and gives nine short case studies of companies that have taken different routes. Available from the Superintendent of Documents at (202) 512-1800.

Weisbord, Marvin, and Sandra Janoff. *Future Search: An Action Guide to Finding Common Ground in Organizations and Communities.* San Francisco: Berrett-Koehler, 1995. A very practical book on how to conduct a Future Search conference. Also, you might be interested in *Discovering Common Ground: How Future Search Conferences Bring People Together to Achieve Breakthrough Innovation, Empowerment, Shared Vision, and Collaborative Action* (San Francisco: Berrett-Koehler, 1992), a series of articles by Weisbord and thirty-five coauthors describing how people have applied Future Search in a variety of settings.

## TOOLS

In *Beyond the Wall of Resistance* I mention a number of approaches that are consistent with the values of the five touchstones—Maintain Clear Focus, Embrace Resistance, Respect Those Who Resist, Relax, Join with the Resistance. My hope is that these tools will serve as a springboard for your own creativity, helping you find ways to apply the touchstones in your organization.

**WORK OUT.** General Electric's way of getting issues worked out (chapter 12).

**FUTURE SEARCH.** This approach gets all stakeholders involved in forming a vision for a new direction (chapters 2, 9, 11, 12; also see Weisbord in the Resources section).

**REAL TIME STRATEGIC CHANGE.** Dannemiller-Tyson's method for getting hundreds actively involved in setting a new direction and developing new procedures (chapters 2, 3, 10, 11; also see Jacobs in Resources).

**DIALOGUE.** This form of communication based on deep attentive listening is at the heart of most approaches. Even used alone it can create dramatic results in shifting people's perceptions of one another (chapter 4; also see Bohm in the Resources section).

**"WHAT IF?" SCENARIOS.** A way to get many groups aligned at the start of a project (chapter 11).

**SEQUENTIAL PROBLEM SOLVING.** Under the section titled "Roll Your Own," I describe a method Washington Gas used to get an entire department involved in decision making using a series of meetings with changing casts of characters (chapter 11).

Also, see the Resources section for details on the book by Laura Spencer for a simple and effective approach to group problem solving and Harrison Owen's book on open-space technology.

# INDEX

ABC, 39

Aboriginal tribe, 52

Action: and acknowledging the old, 175-176; critical mass for, 172-173; and cultural fit, 174; and finding a Marco Polo, 176-177; and going for understanding, 178-179; and key players' support for change, 173-174; knowing when to end, 176; moving without support, 177-178; and offering self as sacrifice, 179; perseverance in, 179, 182; and planning for future change, 182; and reading history, 174-175; signs indicating need for, 172-176; and supporting change agents, 177; timing of, 171-172, 174, 180-181

ADC Kentrox, 27-28

Adizes, Ichak, 193

Advantages of new ideas, 89

Advice seeking, 164

Agreement: easy agreement as resistance, 27-28; in Stalled position, 79, 82-83

Aikido, 25, 60, 165, 176, 193

Al Huang, Chungliang, 167, 170

Alighieri, Dante, 21, 161-162, 193

Allen, Woody, 64, 127

America Online, 89

Anger, 168-169

Animosity, historic, 95-96

Anticipation of future, 68-71

Anticipation of resistance, 29

Appreciative inquiry, 190n2

*Appreciative Management and Leadership* (Cooperrider and Srivastva), 190n2

Arafat, Yasir, 96

Arendt, Hannah, 87

Argyris, Chris, 158-159, 191n1, 193

Armstrong, C. Michael, 173-174

Army Corp of Engineers, 130

Assessment: of balance of forces, 80-81; of everyone's relative position in cycle of change, 75-85; of In It Together position in cycle of change, 79; of intensity of resistance, 87-105; of Level 1 resistance to idea itself, 88-91; of Level 2 resistance involving deeper issues, 91-95; of Level 3 deeply embedded resistance, 95-97; of personal resistance style, 107-119; self-

assessment of personal resistance style, 107-119; of stakeholders in change, 83; of Stalled position in cycle of change, 79, 82-84; Support for Change questionnaire, 97-104; of Way Out Ahead position in cycle of change, 77-79

Athletes, expectations of, 167, 170

Australian aboriginal tribe, 52

*Bad Day at Black Rock,* 64

Badore, Nancy, 192n4

Balance of forces in change, 80-81

Beckhard, Richard, 122

Bellman, Geoffrey, 116-117

Bernstein, Leonard, 177-178

Berra, Yogi, 140

Block, Peter, 62-63, 92, 189n1, 191n1, 193

Body checks for tension, 167

Bohm, David, 52, 193

Bonneville Power Administration, 144-147, 163, 177

Borg-Warner, 124

Branson Ultrasonics, 166

Breathing, 166

Bridges, William, 192n3, 193-194

Buck, Pearl S., 33

Buddhists, 55, 168

Bureaucratic culture, 92

Burroughs, William, 21

Cage, John, 23

Carter, John, 80-81

Carville, James, 166

Catalyst, 188n1

Catherine the Great, 53

Celebration of resistance, 85

Center for Excellence in Government, 144

Champy, James, 18

Change: and acknowledging the old, 175-176; agreement on strategies, 79, 82; assessment of everyone's relative position in cycle of change, 75-85; balance of forces in, 80-81; conflict over strategies, 82-83; conventional approaches to, 40; critical mass for, 172-173; and cultural fit, 174; cycle of, 29-32, 35, 67-71; failed change and resistance, 17-19, 186n5; frantic pace of, 19; and going

for understanding, 178-179; In It Together position in, 79, 125; joining the resistance at beginning of, 60; and key players' support for, 173-174; knowing when to end, 176; and moving against the tide, 75-76; and moving with the tide, 76; moving without support, 177-178; natural change, 50-51; and offering self as sacrifice, 179; perseverance in, 179, 182; planning for future change, 182; and reading history, 174-175; in rules of game at beginning, 60-61; seeds of destruction within cycle of, 70-71, 85; signs indicating time for action on, 172-176; stakeholders in, 82-83, 172-174; Stalled position in, 79, 82-83, 126; Support for Change questionnaire, 97-104; and supporting change agents, 177; timing of, 174, 180-181; unconventional approaches to, 41; as unsettling, 19; Way Out Ahead position in, 77-79, 125-126; Women's Initiative at Deloitte & Touche, 65-73. *See also* Cycle of change; Resistance
Change agents, 52, 90, 177
Changing the game, 60-61
Chaos, and resistance, 47
Chapman, Jan, 135
Chesterton, G. K., 20
Chrysler, 174
Cinmade, 55-56, 78, 178
Civil rights movement, 55, 58
Clarity. *See* Clear Focus
Clark, Karen Kaiser, 56
Clark, Pat, 135, 136
Clear Focus: and engaging resistance with courage, 165; flip side of, 63-64; individual's use of, 70; organization's use of, 72; self-assessment on use of, 118; as touchstone, 54-56; and trust, 137; and unleashing power of resistance, 151
Cleveland baseball stadium, 43-46, 171-172, 176
Clinton, Bill, 150
Cocoon for change agents, 177
*Columbo,* 58
Comedians, and hecklers, 64, 167
Common Ground Network for Life and Choice, 96, 100-101, 133-135
Communication: in digging beneath the surface, 155-159; about new idea, 88-90; as response to resistance, 45; about the undiscussibles, 158-159

Compatibility of new ideas with old way of doing things, 89
Compliance, malicious, 27
CompuServe, 89
Conflict over strategies, 82-83
Conflicting values and visions, 96
Confusion, as resistance, 26
Conner, Daryl, 194
Consultants, and shadow consultant, 163-164
*Consultant's Calling, The* (Bellman), 116
Control, loss of, 113-114
Cook, Mike, 66
Cooke, Jack Kent, 34-35, 37, 186n2
Cooperrider, David, 190n2
Courage. *See* Engaging resistance with courage
Creating the shift to Joining with Resistance: conditions facilitating, 123-125; and cycle of change, 125-126; examples of, 121-122; and In It Together position, 125; and individual visions, 124; and self-disclosure, 124; and shared dissatisfaction, 122-123; and shared meaning, 125; and Stalled position, 126; and telling our stories, 123-124; and Way Out Ahead position, 125-126
Critical mass for action, 172-173
Criticism: immediate criticism as resistance, 26; in-your- face criticism as resistance, 28-29
Crum, Tom, 60-61, 194
Cultural fit, and change, 174
Cycle of change: and anticipation of future, 68-71; assessment of everyone's relative position in, 75-85; and avoiding hoopla, 85; balance of forces in, 80-81; and celebrating resistance, 85; and creating the shift to Joining with Resistance, 125-126; dynamics and nuances of, 83-85; each stage has its day, 83-84; example of resistance and, 35; and holding onto a dying program, 85; Implementation stage of, 31, 68, 109; In It Together position in, 79, 125; Initial Actions stage of, 31, 67-68, 109; Integration stage of, 31; interruptions in, 84-85; and moving against the tide, 75-76; and moving too fast, 83; and moving with the tide, 76; Random Incidents stage of, 31, 60, 67, 108; Recognition stage of, 30, 60, 67, 109; seeds of destruction within, 70-71, 85; stages of, 29-32; Stalled position in, 79, 82-83, 126; Waning Activity stage

of, 31-32; Way Out Ahead position in, 77-79, 125-126; Women's Initiative at Deloitte & Touche as example of, 67-71

D.C. football stadium, 34-35, 37
Dalai Lama, 55
Dannemiller, Kathie, 121-122, 131, 190n1
Dannemiller-Tyson, 121-122, 131
Dante, 21, 161-162, 193
"Dead thing on the table," 141, 158
Deal making, as default position to resistance, 37
Deep breathing, 166
Default positions on software, 187n4
Default positions to resistance, 35-42, 46-57, 107, 112, 142
Defining terms, 155
Definition of resistance, 23-26, 50
Deflection, as resistance, 28
DeGraffenreidt, James, 135, 136
Deloitte & Touche, 65-73, 83, 151, 188n1
Denial, as resistance, 26-27
Denver, John, 60-61
*Detroit Free Press,* 57
Dialogue: and dissipation of resistance, 51-52; structured dialogue, 133-135, 198
*Diffusion of Innovations, The* (Rogers), 89-90
Digging beneath the surface: defining terms, 155; discussing the undiscussibles, 158-159; feedback on impressions, 156, 158; listening and probing, 154-155; listening at different levels, 156; listening between the lines, 155-156; need for, 153; and no interruptions, 156; paraphrasing, 155-156; process for getting things on the table, 157; tools for exploration, 155-159
Dignity, loss of, 93. *See also* Respect
Dissatisfaction, shared, 122-123
Distrust, 92. *See also* Trust
*Doctor Jekyll and Mister Hyde* (Stevenson), 111
Dr. Seuss, 33
Dole, Robert, 167
Downsizing, 40, 187n10, 190-191n2
Du Pont, 35, 44-46
*Duck Soup,* 53-54
Ducks Unlimited, 61

Easy agreement, as resistance, 27-28
Eban, Abba, 17

Edwards, Tilden, 168-169
Embracing Resistance: avoidance of, 113-114; individual's use of, 71; organization's use of, 72; as touchstone, 56- 57; and trust, 137
Emery, Fred, 132
Emery, Merrilyn, 132
*Empowered Manager, The* (Block), 62
Energy, resistance as, 24-25
Energy Department, U.S., 144
Engaging resistance with courage: attributes of guide for, 163; becoming own guide in, 165-167, 170; and Dante's Inferno, 161-162; partnership in, 164; and relaxation, 165-167, 170; and seeking advice, 164; and shadow consultant, 163 164; and teaming up, 164; and touchstones, 165-167, 170; Virgil as guide, 162-165; ways to use guides' wisdom in, 164-165
Environmental groups, 61-62, 144, 180-181
Exercise, 165
Expectations, 167, 170

Failed change, 17-19, 186n5
Faith, and engaging resistance with courage, 166
Fear: creation of, 40; of isolation, 93; of job loss, 93, 94-95, 187n10; of loss of control, 113-114; as opposite of trust, 128-129
Feedback in advance, 146-148
Feedback on impressions, 156, 158
Fisher, Anne B., 18
Fisher, Roger, 194
*Flawless Consulting* (Block), 62
Focus groups, 149
Focusing: and engaging resistance with courage, 165; flip side of, 63-64; to get beyond wall of resistance, 54-56; individual's use of, 70; organization's use of, 72; self- assessment on use of, 118; and trust, 137; and unleashing power of resistance, 151
Folly, of leaders, 49, 50-51
Force of reason, as default position to resistance, 36-37
Ford, Henry, 80
Ford, Henry II, 174
Ford Motor Company, 121-122, 124, 174, 176, 190n2, 192n4
*Foundations for Change,* 207
Fram oil filters, 127

Frey, Robert, 55-56, 78, 178, 194
Future: anticipation of, by using cycle of change, 68-71; planning for, 182
Future Search, 132-133, 176, 198

Gabriel, Ellen, 66, 188n1
Game theory, 39-40, 187n9
Gandhi, Mahatma, 107
Gateway Center, 44
GE, 142-143
Gestalt Institute of Cleveland, 188n2, 194
Gestalt psychology, 194
*Getting Things Done When You Are Not in Charge* (Bellman), 116
Gibb, Jack, 128
Gingrich, Newt, 167
Giving in too soon, as default position to resistance, 38
Glasow, Arnold, 75
Goldwyn, Samuel, 129
Goodman, Michael, 48
Grant, Felix, 89
*Green Eggs and Ham* (Dr. Seuss), 33
*Grunt, The,* 140-141
Gunnersfield Ranch, 61

Halifax, Lord, 171
Hammer, Michael, 18
Hanh, Thich Nhat, 194
Harbridge House, 188nn1-2
Harvey, Rose, 180-181
*Healing and the Mind,* 26-27
*Healing the Wounds* (Noer), 187n10, 190-191n2
Hecklers, and comedians, 64, 167
Herodotus, 128
Historic animosity, 95-96
History, 174-175
Hoffer, Eric, 161
Honesty, 58-59, 129
Hughes Aircraft, 173-174
Humor, 167, 172-173
Huxley, Aldous, 139

*I Ching,* 194-195
Iacocca, Lee, 174
IBM, 31, 186n5
Ideas: communication about, 88-90; compatibility of new ideas with old way of doing things, 89; as easy to test, 89; involvement

in new ideas, 90; Level 1 resistance to idea itself, 88-91; observability of new ideas, 89-90; relative advantage of new ideas, 89; simplicity of new ideas, 89
Ignoring resistance, as default position, 37
Implementation stage of change, 31, 68, 109
In It Together position in cycle of change, 79, 125
In-your-face criticism, as resistance, 28-29
*Inferno, The* (Dante), 161-162
Inge, William, 15
Initial Actions stage of change, 31, 67-68, 109
Innovations: acceptance or rejection of, 52; Level 1 resistance to idea itself, 88-91
Integration stage of change, 31
Intensity of resistance: degrees of intensity, 87-88; dialogue about, using the Support for Change questionnaire, 97-99; interplay of levels, 97; interpretation of Support for Change questionnaires, 99, 102-103; Level 1 resistance to idea itself, 88-91; Level 2 resistance involving deeper issues, 91-95; Level 3 deeply embedded resistance, 95-97; Level 4 resistance, 189n8; Support for Change questionnaire, 104-105
International Standards Organization, 27-28, 186n2
Interruptions, 156
Involvement in new ideas, 90
ISO 9000 standards, 27-28, 186n2
Isolation, fear of, 93

Jacksteit, Mary, 100-101, 195
Jacobs, Robert, 191n4, 195-196
Jacobs Field, 43-46
James, William, 121
Janoff, Sandra, 197
Japan, 174
Job loss: and downsizing, 187n10; fear of, 93, 94-95
Johnson, Peter, 144-147, 163, 164, 195
Joining with the Resistance: creating shift to, 121-126; organization's use of, 73; self-assessment on use of, 118; as touchstone, 60-63, 64; and trust, 137
Jong, Erica, 153

Karp, Hank, 195
Kaufmann, Adrienne, 100-101, 195
Kayhoe, Matt, 189n9

Kelly, Walt, 107
Kenney, David, 27-28
Killing the messenger, as default position
    to resistance, 37-38

Labor Department, U.S., 197
Language, linear nature of, 48
Lao-tzu, 195
Laughter, 167
*Leadership and the New Science* (Wheatley), 50
Level 1 resistance to idea itself, 88-91
Level 2 resistance involving deeper issues,
    91-95
Level 3 deeply embedded resistance, 95-97
Level 4 resistance, 189n8
Linear view: of language, 48; of resistance,
    46-47
Lippitt, Ron, 124, 132
Listening: at different levels, 156; in digging
    beneath the surface, 154-156; listening
    between the lines, 155-156; with no inter-
    ruptions, 156; and respect, 58
Long view, as response to resistance, 46, 55
Loss of control, fear of, 113-114
Loss of face, 93. *See also* Respect
Loss of respect, 93. *See also* Respect
Louis XIV, 50
Lynch, Jerry, 167, 170

Machiavelli, Niccolò, 36
Mahler, Gustav, 177-178
Maintaining Clear Focus: and engaging
    resistance with courage, 165; flip side
    of, 63-64; individual's use of, 70; organi-
    zation's use of, 72; self-assessment on
    use of, 118; as touchstone, 54-56; and
    trust, 137; and unleashing power of
    resistance, 151
Making deals, as default position to resis-
    tance, 37
Malicious compliance, as resistance, 27
*Managing Organizational Transitions*
    (Bridges), 192n3
Manipulation: as default position to resis-
    tance, 36; and undiscussibles, 159
Mao, Chairman, 55
*March of Folly, The* (Tuchman), 50-51
Martin, Lynn, 66
Marx, Groucho, 26, 53-54
Maurer, Rick, 13

Maurer & Associates, 207
McGagen, Doug, 61
McKinsey and Company, 18, 185n2
Meaning, shared, 125
Meditation, 165, 168-169
Mergers, failure of, 18, 185n2
Middle Eastern politics, 96
Mount Saint Helens, 139-140
Moving against the tide, 75-76
Moving with the tide, 76
Moyers, Bill, 26-27
Murphy, Tom, 188n1
Mutual gain, as response to resistance, 46

Nappo, Liz, 166
Natural change, 50-51
Natural Resources Defense Council, 144
Nature Conservancy, 61
Nature of resistance, 23-32, 140-141
Nevis, Edwin, 58, 195-196
New ideas, resistance to, 88-91
Newspaper, underground, 140-141
Nixon, Richard, 129
Noer, David, 187n10, 190-191n2, 196
Nuclear arms reduction, 129

Observability of new ideas, 89-90
Oestreich, Daniel, 196
Orr, Marshall, 191n3
Owen, Harrison, 196

Pando Clone, 52
Paradox of resistance, 25-26, 186n6
Paraphrasing, 155
Partnership, in engaging resistance with
    courage, 164
*Patton,* 187n8
Penn and Teller, 167
Perseverance, 55, 162, 165, 176, 179, 182. See
    also Maintaining Clear Focus
Personal resistance style, self-assessment of,
    107-119
Pilots' Union, 179
Planning for future change, 182
Playing off relationships, as default position
    to resistance, 37
*Pogo,* 107
Polo, Marco, 176-177
*Poseidon Adventure, The,* 39
Potential in resistance, 43-52

Power: and folly of leaders, 49, 50-51; of resistance, 17- 22; unleashing power of resistance, 139-151; use of, as default position to resistance, 36; of volcanoes, 139- 140
Practice, for engaging resistance with courage, 165-166
Price Waterhouse, 196
*Prince, The* (Machiavelli), 36
Problem-solving process, 135-138, 200
Prodigy, 89
Protection, resistance as, 24
Public Involvement Policy, 144-147, 163
Punishments and rewards, and resistance, 93
Pyrrhus, 39
Pythagoras, 25

Quality circles, 32
Quality improvement process, 70-71, 135, 174, 186n4
Questionnaires: informal questionnaires for unleashing power of resistance, 149; Support for Change questionnaire, 97-104

Rabin, Yitzhak, 96
Random Incidents stage of change, 30, 56, 60, 108
Real Time Strategic Change, 122, 131-132, 176, 191n4, 198
Reason, as default position to resistance, 36-37
Recognition of resistance, 26-29
Recognition stage of change, 30, 60, 67, 109
Reed, William, 60
Reengineering, 18, 24
*Reengineering the Corporation* (Hammer and Champy), 18
Reisner, Mark, 61
Relationships. *See* Playing off relationships
Relaxation: before meeting with others, 165-166; and deep breathing, 166; during meeting with others, 166-167, 170; and engaging resistance with courage, 165-167, 170; and exercise, 165; and faith in higher purpose, 166; flip side of, 64; individual's use of, 71; and knowing intentions of those who resist, 59-60; and laughter, 167; organization's use of, 73; and practice, 165-166; self-assessment on use of, 118; and sleep, 165; as touchstone,

59-60, 64; and trust, 137; and unleashing power of resistance, 150-151; while staying engaged, 59
Resilience, 94
Resistance: anticipating, 29; celebration of, 85; challenge of, 19; conventional approaches to, 35-42, 46- 47, 53-54, 142; and creating the shift, 121-126; and cycle of change, 29-32; default positions to, 35-42, 46- 47, 53-54, 107, 112, 142; definition of, 23-26, 50; digging beneath surface of, 153-159; as energy, 24-25; engaging resistance with courage, 161-170; and failed dreams, 17-18; and human toll of failed change, 19; ignoring, 37; image of wall of, 19; increasing resistance by making matters worse, 33-42, 53-54; intensity of, 87-105; Level 1 resistance to idea itself, 88-91; Level 2 resistance involving deeper issues, 91-95; Level 3 deeply embedded resistance, 95-97; Level 4 resistance, 189n8; nature of, 23-32, 140-141; paradox of, 25-26, 186n6; potential in, 43-52; power of, 17-22; preempting, 127-138; as protection, 24; questions for exploration of, 48-49; recognizing, 26-29; resources on, 193-198; in spiritual journeys, 168-169; strong reaction to, 33-35, 53-54; Support for Change questionnaire, 97- 104; touchstones for getting beyond the wall, 53-64; unconventional approaches to, 41, 45-52; and the unknown, 57; unleashing, 139-151; value of working with, 20-22. *See also* Change
Respect: flip side of, 63-64; and honesty, 58-59; individual's use of, 70-71; and listening with interest, 58; loss of respect and Level 2 resistance involving deeper issues, 93; organization's use of, 72; as response to resistance, 45; self-assessment on use of, 118; struggle for, 57-58; as touchstone, 57-59; and unleashing power of resistance, 150; versus trust, 58
Respecting Those Who Resist: flip side of, 63-64; individual use of, 70-71; organization's use of, 72; self-assessment on use of, 118; as touchstone, 57-59; and trust, 137; and unleashing power of resistance, 150
Restroom talk, 141, 191n1
Rewards and punishments, and resistance, 93
Rice growers, 61-62

Ricelands Habitat Partnership, 61
Richards, Lloyd, 142, 163
Robertson, Jack, 17, 144-147, 163, 164
Rogers, Everett, 52, 89-90, 196
Rowan, Hobart, 57
Ryan, Kathleen, 196

Sabotage, as resistance, 27
Sacrifice, 179
Sales, 56-57, 88
Samurai warriors, 60
Schindler-Rainman, Eva, 132
Schutz, Will, 191n2
Schwarzenegger, Arnold, 59
Seeking advice, 164
Self-assessment of personal resistance style:
    avoiding embracing resistance, 113-114;
    Bellman on, 116-117; changes in style for
    improvement, 115-116; considering past
    change that failed, 108-109; external
    reactions to others' resistance, 112; feel-
    ings, 110-111; identifying personal strate-
    gies that use the touchstones, 117-118;
    impact of reactions to others' resistance,
    112-113; importance of, 107-108; internal
    reactions to others' resistance, 110-111;
    key questions on current reactions to oth-
    ers' resistance, 119; others' resistance to
    change, 109-110; patterns in reaction to
    others' resistance, 114- 115; physical
    reactions, 111; thoughts, 110
Self-disclosure, 124, 133
Separation from others, 41-42
Sequential problem solving, 135-138, 198
Set point, 24
Seuss, Dr., 33
Shadow consultants, 163-164
Shalem Institute for Spiritual Formation,
    168-169
Shared dissatisfaction, and creating the shift,
    122-123
Shared meaning, and creating the shift, 125
Shift. See Creating the shift
Short view, for getting beyond wall of resis-
    tance, 55
Silence: as resistance, 28; and transformation, 169
Simplicity of new ideas, 89
Sleep, 165
Snow, Tony, 57
Soft eyes, 188n2

Software applications, failure of, 18
Soviet Union, 129, 150
Spencer, Laura, 196
Sperlich, Harold, 174
Spiritual journeys, 168-169
Srivastva, Suresh, 190n2
Stahlman, Mark, 31
Stakeholders in change, 82-83, 172-174
Stalled position in cycle of change, 79, 82-83, 126
Standish Group, 18
Stark, Max, 188n12
Stevenson, Robert Louis, 111
*Stewardship* (Block), 62
Storytelling, 123-124
Structured dialogue, 133-135, 198
Support for Change questionnaire: dialogue
    using, 97-99; form, 104-105; interpreta-
    tion of, 99, 102-103
Surveys, for unleashing power of resistance,
    148-149
Suspicion, creation of, 40
Synergy, failure to create, 40

T'ai Chi, 59, 197
Taiwan chemical plant, 44-46
Telling our stories, 123-124
Tension: body checks for, 167; and limited
    vision, 60. *See also* Relaxation
*Thinking Body, Dancing Mind* (Lynch and
    Al Huang), 167, 170
Tibetan Buddhists, 55, 168
Timing of change, 171-172, 174, 180-181
Tolstoy, Leo, 107
Total quality management, 70-71
Touchstones for getting beyond wall of resis-
    tance: Embrace Resistance, 56-57, 71, 72,
    118, 137; and engaging resistance with
    courage, 165-167, 170; flip side of, 62- 64;
    individual's use of, 70-71; Join with the
    Resistance, 60-63, 64, 72, 118, 137;
    Maintain Clear Focus, 54-56, 63- 64, 70,
    72, 118, 137, 151, 165; organization's use
    of, 72-73; Relax, 59-60, 64, 71, 73, 118,
    137, 150-151, 165- 167, 170; reminders of,
    166; Respect Those Who Resist, 57-59, 63-
    64, 70-71, 72, 118, 137, 150; self-assess-
    ment in use of, 117-118; and trust, 137;
    and unleashing power of resistance, 150;
    and "What If?" scenarios, 131; Women's
    Initiative at Deloitte & Touche, 72-73

TPL. See Trust for Public Land (TPL)

Tracy, Spencer, 64

Trust: dilemma of, 128-130; distrust and Level 2 resistance, 92; fear as opposite of, 128-129; and honesty, 129; and self-disclosure, 124, 133; and touchstones, 137; and verify, 129-130; versus respect, 58

Trust for Public Land (TPL), 180-181

Tuchman, Barbara, 49, 50-51

20th Century Fox, 39

Underground newspaper, 140-141

Understanding of change, 178-179

Undiscussibles, 141, 158-159

United Airlines, 179

United Auto Workers, 122

U.S. Army Corp of Engineers, 130

U.S. Congress, 37

U.S. Department of Energy, 144

U.S. Department of Labor, 197

Unknown, and resistance, 57

Unleashing power of resistance: asking people directly for reactions to change, 142-143; focus groups, 149; and informal questionnaires, 149; inviting the storm, 141-151; making it easy for people to speak, 148; principles for, 150-151; Public Involvement Policy, 144-146; reasons for, 140; reviewing formal surveys, 148-149; soliciting feedback in advance, 146-148; and touchstones, 150-151; and volcano's power, 139-140; and warning signs of resistance, 140-141; Workout Program, 142-143

Ury, William, 194, 196

Values, conflicting, 96

Vienna Philharmonic, 177-178

Vietnam War, 37-38

Virgil as guide for engaging resistance, 162-170

Vision: conflicting visions and Level 3 deeply embedded resistance, 96; individual visions and creating the shift, 124; and shared dissatisfaction, 122-123

Volcanoes, 139-140

Wagner, Jane, 70

Wall, Jim, 188n1

Wall of resistance. See Resistance

Waning Activity stage of change, 31-32

Washington, D.C. football stadium, 34-35, 37

Washington Gas, 135-138

Way Out Ahead position in cycle of change, 77-79, 125-126

Weisbord, Marvin, 132-133, 197

Welch, Jack, 142-143

"What If?" scenarios, 130-131, 198

What's in it for me? question, 48, 57-58, 60, 128

What's in it for them? question, 48-49, 60, 68-69, 128, 154-155

What's in it for us? question, 49, 60-62

Wheatley, Margaret, 50-51

Wilde, Oscar, 43

Wilder, Douglas, 34-35, 37

Win, cost of, 39

Win-lose mind set, 38-39

Wolf, Stephen, 179

Women's Initiative at Deloitte & Touche, 65-73, 188nn1-2

Workout Program, 142-143, 198

World events, and resistance, 94

Worsening the situation, by increasing resistance, 33-42, 54-55

Wright, Robert, 57

Yeltsin, Boris, 150

Yin and yang, 25-26

Yoga, 165

Zenger Miller, 18

Zero-sum games, 39-40, 61

## MAURER & ASSOCIATES

Maurer & Associates helps organizations implement change while paying attention to people. They work closely with clients to develop strategies that build support for change. They are experienced in large-systems change interventions, executive coaching, building alliances between departments, team building, and management development.

Since 1978, the firm has advised and trained executives as well as line and staff managers and workers in business, industry, government, and academic institutions. Its broad range of client organizations has included Bell Atlantic, Fannie Mae (Federal National Home Mortgage), MCI, Tulane Medical Center, the International Monetary Fund, and the District of Columbia Public Schools.

The firm also publishes a newsletter, *Foundations for Change,* as a way to stimulate thinking on the issues addressed in this book. The newsletter offers examples of change management strategies that adhere to the principles in this book, and continually attempts to explore new ways of building support for change. They may take the newsletter on-line in the near future in order to provide an informal forum for people to learn from each other and test their new ideas.

Rick Maurer is the firm's founder and president. You can contact him at

Maurer & Associates
Phone (703) 525-7074
Fax (703) 525-0183
E-mail: rmaurer@beyondresistance.com
Website: www.beyondresistance.com